**Franchising and network marketing –
are they both winners?**

**Can you truly get wealthy
from a standing start?**

How much risk are you taking?

Is there longterm growth?

**All these questions, and many more,
are answered in . . .**

BOOM BUSINESS
OF THE 90'S

This easy-to-read, informative book shows exactly how anyone can start their own low-risk, low-cost business – with the potential of making a fortune.

Experts in the field have given the book overwhelming praise:

Brilliantly simple, and gives all the basics for success. It is by far the best introduction to the subject. Start reading, and you won't be able to put it down . . .

Sir Michael Grylls, MP, Chairman, Small Business Bureau.

ABOUT THE AUTHOR

Francis Hitching has been writing books, magazine and newspaper articles, and television programs all his working life.

After a successful career in London's Fleet Street, he moved to TV where he originated and produced the legendary rock program *Ready, Steady, Go!*

His first book, *Earth Magic*, was an inquiry into the origins of Stonehenge and other megalithic monuments. He wrote and produced a major TV documentary based on its findings.

His international bestseller, *The World Atlas of Mysteries*, sold more than 500,000 copies worldwide. Many of the topics were adapted and produced by him for the award winning TV series *In Search Of . . .* narrated by Leonard Nimoy, which was shown in 22 countries and is still being aired in the US.

His account of the debate about Darwinism, *The Neck of the Giraffe*, was chosen as Book of the Year by the Nobel prize winner William Golding, and by the acclaimed novelist John Updike. It was selected as Book of the Month by *Reader's Digest*, and was also condensed in *Life* Magazine. A two-part BBC-TV documentary based on it, and narrated by him, is widely used in English High Schools.

Francis Hitching's gift as a documentary writer is to go to the heart of a complex subject and make it plain and readable. In *Boom Business of the 90's*, he gives a balanced account of how to profit from today's universal concern about our polluted environment and its effect on our personal health.

BOOM BUSINESS OF THE 90's

THE ESSENTIAL START-UP GUIDE TO CREATING PERSONAL WEALTH

By Francis Hitching

USER FRIENDLY TEXTBOOKS

Published by User Friendly Textbooks, Swalcliffe Manor, Swalcliffe, Banbury, Oxfordshire, England OX 15 5EH.

To order this book in the United States please phone Toll Free 1-800-347-3172.

First published in the US in June 1994.

Library of Congress Data - A catalogue record for this book is available from the Library of Congress.

ISBN 1-898314-02-0

Text processing and type design by PanSet Arts, Idenden House, Medway Street, Maidstone, Kent, ME14 1JT.

Cover design by Tony Stocks Graphics, 15 Nassau Street, London, W1N 7RE.

Printed and bound in the United Kingdom by Mackays of Chatham PLC, Badger Road, Lordswood, Chatham, Kent ME5 8TD.

CONTENTS

ACKNOWLEDGMENTS

Franchising and network marketing are cousins. They share a philosophy: *you're in business for yourself, but not by yourself.* In other words, you're your own boss, but you get help from the shared experience of everyone in a similar field.

This is, of course, the opposite of the secretive world of corporate business, where somebody else bosses you around, and you must compete ruthlessly with your colleagues if you're going to climb the financial ladder.

I discovered this truth about franchising and network marketing when I began to research this book. I expected the usual difficulties and evasions. Instead, people were completely open: they gave up their time, encouraged me, and showed me how the systems worked.

It was the same on both sides of the Atlantic. The International Franchise Association, based in Washington, DC, freely offered time and information. The UK equivalent is the British Franchise Asssociation, which was equally helpful.

Network marketing comes under the umbrella of the US Direct Selling Association, also in Washington, DC, where I am indebted to George Hescott, who gave invaluable background information on the history and current performance of this form of marketing, and the DSA's permission for me to use the material on pyramiding on pages 27–29. In England, I was similarly helped by Richard Berry, Director of the UK Direct Selling Association.

Finally, I am grateful to the many successful entrepreneurs whose stories are printed in this book, and to all the others whose stories had to be omitted for reasons of space. I would particularly like to thank three of the foremost names in European network marketing, Shay O'Brien, Geoff Liberman, and David Hunt, who were endlessly patient with my initial manuscript, and to Jim Elliott in the US for his guidance in this substantially rewritten version.

Chapter 1

BOOM BUSINESS

In a roving career as author and TV producer, I have involved myself in a major growth industry each decade of my working life.

In the 60s, it was the revolution in pop music. I put together a rock program called *Ready, Steady, Go!* Week after week on British TV screens, we introduced groups and singers who soon became household names: the Beatles, the Rolling Stones, the Who, Jimi Hendrix, the Moody Blues . . .

In the 70s, I became fascinated in ancient mysteries, as did millions of readers and viewers in the United States and around the world: what happened at Stonehenge? was there a Loch Ness monster? a Bermuda Triangle? did flying saucers exist? A hit TV series, *In Search Of . . .*, and a publishing bestseller arose from my researches.

In the 80s I continued to fly back and forth across the Atlantic. In the US, I saw a momentous trend – the mass immigration of Hispanics from Latin America. With colleagues from UCLA, Los Angeles, I put together a multi-media language-learning package to help them learn to speak English and discover what life in the US is like.

Around the same time, I began to gather information about what seemed to me the biggest issue of the coming decade – one I wanted to become engaged with and write about in the 90s. Globally, people were becoming concerned and confused about what was happening to the environment they lived in, and what it was doing to their health.

The media were giving the subject increasing promi-
nence. You could hardly pick up a newspaper or magazine, or watch a TV news program, without some new
item of concern. There were ongoing problems with the
destruction of the rain forests and the ozone layer; dis-
asters like Chernobyl; rivers so poisoned with industrial
waste that no creature could survive in them; office
blocks being demolished because they suffered from
something called "sick building syndrome"; supermarket
foods being banned because of chemical additives.

But what to write about this? What, indeed, could any
individual do? The problems were vast, diffuse. It was
all so negative. Governments paid lip service, and did
little. "Green" parties were formed in most countries in
the Western world, thrived briefly, and then were swal-
lowed by the whales when it came to election time.

A way forward

Gradually, a solution emerged. Well, "solution" is too
strong a word. But at least it offered a way forward, and
was positive. If you couldn't do much about the problems at an international or national or even local level,
because there were so many of them andthe commercial
pressures were so great, perhaps you could do something
individually. You could have a go at cleaning up the
placeswhere you lived and worked – your home, your office – and you could try eating more healthily.

And if you turned from the front page stories about
pollution to the financial pages about how to make
money from it, it was clear that big business was coming
to the same conclusion. According to a market research
study, sales of point-of-use water treatment systems
would grow to $2.5 billion in the mid-90s. Sales of air
treatment systems might be four times that figure.

Throughout America's shopping malls, there was evidence in front of your eyes that people were taking their
diet seriously. Health food stores and supermarket
shelves were brimming with an array of vitamins and

nutritional supplements. Weight watching became a national business, juicing a billion dollar craze.

US citizens, without doubt, were responding to environmental challenge with their purses.

But this still wasn't enough for a story. Big business and politicians mess things up. Ordinary families pay for it. Big business profits. So what's new?

Then, by chance, I was told by a friend about a woman who seemed to have bucked the system. Instead of paying, she earned. I rang her, then met her. The story of what happened to Cheryl Cortese is so remarkable, so heart-warming, and so hopeful for the rest of us, that I print it here mostly in her own words.

* * *

In December 1987, any of Cheryl's friends would have told you she had the perfect family life. Smiling, happy, attractive, married 25 years to a man who had become senior vice president of a major oil company, she lived in a 3,500 sq. ft. home in the most prestigious part of Thibodaux, Louisiana (pop. 15,000).

Her son Christopher, 19, was in college. Her daughter Edith, 17, looked forward to following him. Cheryl, a homemaker and nursery teacher while her children were growing up, was by then a lecturer at Nicholls State University.

That month, the bottom fell out of her world.

It happened so suddenly. Our marriage had been having a few midlife difficulties, but nothing that I thought wasn't handleable. Then one day, out of the blue, my husband announced he was finished with being married. He wanted to go his own way, and that was that. No argument. Final.

I was terrified and bewildered. I was 18 when we married, so I'd known no other life. Now this. I'd always had a private nightmare of whether I could cope if I had to look after myself - and here it was, the nightmare come true.

The lawyers moved in. Cheryl blames them for a lot of the bitterness and anger that followed. The house went to her husband. Cheryl had to move to an apartment in New Orleans.

I felt so hopeless and guilty that I didn't even have the courage to tell my friends we were divorcing. Then a friend of a friend heard what was happening and made an appointment to see me.

I remember him saying that money's not a cure for everything, but it sure helps with the logistics. He tried to put my mind at rest. He told me about something called network marketing, and said it involved distributing environmentally friendly products. The main one was a treatment system that made water taste good in the home - no chlorine, just like bottled water. Then, for two weeks, he helped me put the word about and get on the phone and tell everyone I ever knew that I was setting up a new business, and that it was an opportunity they might be interested in, too.

Setting a goal

It was therapy, as much as anything else. I didn't see it as the answer, not then. One of my biggest fears was not having medical insurance any more. I found out that if I reached a certain level in his networking company, free insurance was included. So that became my goal.

I still didn't properly understand how the business worked, but the literature was good, and there was always someone on the end of a helpline. So I just carried right on, learning as I went. I must have talked to more than 300 people in that first month. It was December going into January, so I didn't have to use up time in the university job.

For the month's work, I had a paycheck from the company for $15,771.60. I'll never forget the figure. Compare it with teaching, which gave me $17,000 a year at best. It was incredible. So I kept working in the new business, and every month afterward I averaged $12,000-$15,000 net.

Eight months on, I reached the position where I got my free insurance, and a lot else besides. Within 18 months, I had passive earnings large enough that it didn't matter whether I worked or not. I had no problems paying for my children to go through college. After three years, I had a seven figure income, and it's stayed that way.

I believe network marketing saved my life, in every sense. I'm still a teacher - this time showing people how to make a difference in their own lives. Truly, I love the way I live.

*   *   *

A seven-figure income in three years? From someone who started from rock-bottom with no business experience and almost no money? Like anyone else hearing this sort of story for the first time, I initially thought it unbelievable.

But the bank statements and the computer printouts were there to prove it, and I promise that every word in Cheryl's story, checked again and again, is true.

Through Cheryl, I discovered the power of network marketing - and her climb to success is the best possible introduction to this book. In an age when huge corporations still dominate most of our lives, it is still possible, thank God, to be a successful and benevolent entrepreneur. Network marketing and franchising are the two most popular routes.

So how do you go about it? And which should be your choice?

Chapter 2

TO GOOD TO BE TRUE?

I guess we all know something about the power of franchising. It's huge. One out of every three dollars spent by Americans for goods and services is spent in a franchised business. In 1990, the total number of franchises in the US achieved the milestone of half a million, and it has grown each year since. Currently, a new franchise opens every six and a half minutes. Eight million jobs depend on it.

What's more, if you're looking to work for yourself for the first time, it's fairly safe and dependable. Banks look sympathetically at requests for initial financing loans. Whereas six in ten independent startup businesses fail in their first five years, more than nine out of ten franchise businesses succeed. There is money to be made. A Gallup survey suggested that the average gross income before tax of franchisees exceeds $120,000 a year.

But . . .

- To get hold of a franchise, you have to invest a lot of your own money – saved, borrowed, or both. The minimum will probably be close to $50,000 (whatever the ads say), and that won't get you much more than a one-van business. If you want the kind of money Cheryl Cortese achieves, you may need three or four franchises at $500,000 each.

- Only a tiny proportion of the franchises on offer are related to the demand for an environmental and health cleanup which I believe to be the true boom business of the 90s.

With network marketing, the position is reversed. Your entry money will be less than $75, and even after buying some stock and tools of the trade, the maximum investment in your first month should not exceed $1,500.

Yet a significant number of people manage to turn this tiny investment, in three to five years, into a fortune. As the title of this chapter suggests, it seems too good to be true.

I don't blame anyone for being skeptical, says Cheryl Cortese. *I was, to begin with.*

So was I. So is almost everyone, when they first hear of it. I asked a few friends for their reactions. Typically, they went something like this:

> *It's that old pyramid, chain-letter thing, isn't it?*

> *It's all about wives drinking coffee and selling each other household stuff, isn't it?*

> *I had a cousin who tried it, and it didn't work.*

On both sides of the Atlantic, I found phrases about network marketing occurring again and again. *Pyramids, garages full of junk, it's a scam, I'm not a salesperson . . .* the misunderstandings seem to be universal.

As with most instant reactions, there are distant truths to back them up. About 20 years ago, dishonest pyramid salesmen found a way of attaching themselves to network marketing, which in itself is an entirely ethical business concept. Amid much publicity, pyramidselling was outlawed – but the memory lingers on.

Historically, too, network marketing began in a small way through the sharing of vitamin products among friends. And of course, it is true that some people fail in network marketing – certainly more than in franchising.

But the old-fashioned image of network marketing is no longer a reality. Because I want to put the current situation in perspective, this book is more about network marketing than about franchising (although a later chapter will examine one of the health food franchises as a possible business opportunity.) For the fact is that whatever happened in the past, network marketing has got its act together.

Anyone who would like to have an extra profit center, or is thinking of a career change that might lead to serious wealth, would be well advised to take a closer look at what's happening. *Megatrends* author John Naisbitt wrote that *franchising is the single most successful marketing concept ever.* I myself would say that in its own way, *network marketing is the most effective method yet invented of starting your own company from zero.*

First, some facts. Network marketing, in one form or another, has been around for at least 50 years. Usually, it has been called Multi Level Marketing, or MLM.

Yet relatively few people seem to have recognized just how dramatic its growth has been in recent times. Worldwide, network marketing has defied recession, and is currently doubling in size about every five years. In 1993, global sales in 36 countries approached $40 billion.

Japan led with about $13 billion in sales. The US was not far behind with $10 billion, achieved through more than 3 million independent distributors. Seven other countries – Brazil, Canada, France, Germany, Italy, Taiwan, and the UK – each generated more than $1 billion in sales.

Distinguished outside observers see the trend continuing. Lord William Rees-Mogg, former editor of the London *Times,* renowned for the accuracy of his world economic forecasts, says in his book *The Great Reckoning* that as regular jobs decrease, more and more households will look to network marketing to earn additional income.

Faith Popcorn, another recognized forecaster from New York, NY, says in her book *The Popcorn Report* that selling in the home will increase while sales in shopping malls decline. It will be the next consumer-oriented revolution. She identifies as the next phase: *direct shopping from the producer to you – bypassing the retailer altogether, no middlemen, no stops along the way.*

Success stories abound: of companies which have adopted the system and are now turning over hundreds of $ millions a year; of individuals who have made enough money to retire after only two or three years; of thousands of others who have freed themselves from financial worries for the first time in their lives. Uniquely:

ANYONE CAN PROFIT FROM NETWORK MARKETING, BECAUSE:

* You don't need sales skills

* You can do it part-time

* You don't need prior business experience (but you must be teachable)

ANYONE CAN START THEIR OWN LOW-RISK BUSINESS, BECAUSE:

* You don't need a big investment

* Your overheads will be virtually nil

* You don't employ staff (and you don't have a boss)

* You can make immediate income

* You learn the business while you earn

THE POTENTIAL IS LIMITLESS, BECAUSE:

* The more you learn and teach, the more people will succeed alongside you

* Your organization can grow as large as you choose

* The bigger your organization grows, the more money everyone makes

Now whether you are hearing about networking for the first or the umpteenth time, these are large claims. Particularly when you may also be told that for 5–15 hours per week part-time, you may make $10–20,000 profit per year. And that, full-time, there is no reason why you shouldn't make the same amount *per month*. Since the average annual wage in the US is around $30,000, and most of us only ever read in the newspapers about people making monthly figures in this range, it would be surprising if you didn't raise an eyebrow in disbelief.

But the fact is that the success stories are true. I have talked to more than a hundred people with incomes to prove it: they were students, teachers, housewives;

WHY WAIT?

Sue Burdick started a network marketing business that has brought herself and husband Bob a string of horses and a 90-acre farm in Georgia.

Bob was a carpenter. I had five sons and six grandchildren. There wasn't much money around, so I decided to go find a way to contribute. A friend told me about network marketing, but I was fixed in my mind that I ought to go back to school to get myself some qualifications. What a mistake!

I learned real estate. Didn't suit me. Tried computer school. Too difficult. Then a dog-grooming disaster. Couldn't handle the fleas. Taught aerobics. Too much sweat. So I washed windows, did cleaning jobs.

Then the idea of networking came up again. I borrowed $300 and tried it – and for the first time here was something that worked. I earned more than Bob in my very first month. So he put carpentry on one side and joined me.

A year later, we bought back a home we had lost. In six and a half years, we have become millionaires. Nowadays, if anyone says to me they'll think about network marketing for a while before signing up, I just say "Why wait?"

people who have been made redundant, or whose businesses failed, or who successfully sold up what they were doing to get in on the opportunity; bankers, accountants, doctors, dentists, nurses; builders, blue-collar workers, managers, salespeople – all these and many more.

There seems no common denominator except the general rule that *anyone can learn to do it*.

Time and energy

Nobody who presents you with an honest picture of network marketing will pretend that achieving such results is easy, let alone automatic. It means setting up a distribution network in which a large number of people do a little each. That takes time and energy. It is also true that only a small proportion hit the heights.

But there are many advantages, one of which is that you choose who you want to work with. All you do is find a handful of friends, colleagues, or business associates who you feel would like the opportunity to distribute a range of products you all believe to be worthwhile. Then they in turn find some more people to do the same thing. Gradually (or quite quickly, if you work hard) the number of distributors will grow.

Before long, you may find yourself with an organization of hundreds, or even thousands, of people like yourself. As a reward for having worked hard, and helping these people, the company will pay you, monthly, a percentage override on group turnover. It's not difficult – and shouldn't be costly – to get started. You should make some money from the beginning: learn as you earn, the saying goes. Secondary incomes of $500–$1,000+ per month are common.

After that, it takes time, patience, understanding, teaching, and enthusiasm to lead your organization into a significant size – just the same as building any business. Above all, it takes persistence. There is a significant dropout rate from those who show lack of commitment, and become disheartened by slow results. Inevitably, some such people will be in your organization, and you will have to work to make sure you give them the help they need, and if necessary replace them.

But the pot of gold is there for those who keep at it. Any well-established network marketing company can provide documentary evidence that their top earners, after two or three years in the business, are making more than $200,000 a year – in some cases, several times that.

Network marketing is about making dreams come true. You can dream about getting yourself out of a financial hole; or about buying the house or car or boat you always wanted; or not having to commute; or not having a boss; or having enough money to stop work altogether in 3–5 years' time. You can dream of developing enough self-confidence to take charge of your life, and not be dependent on others. With consistent effort, many ordinary people have achieved all this, and more.

Their guiding principle is so profoundly simple that you can only wonder why it's not better known:

YOU CAN MAKE A LIVING MARKETING A PRODUCT. BUT YOU CAN MAKE A FORTUNE BY BUILDING A NETWORK AND TEACHING OTHERS TO DO THE SAME

Chapter 3

2 + 3 = 781

The purpose of network marketing is the same as with any other method of marketing: to distribute as much product as possible from the manufacturer to the end-user. Network marketing is growing explosively because, with the right products, companies are finding it does the job so well.

Here, typically, is why:

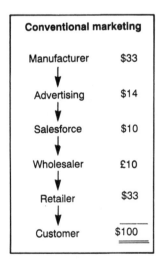

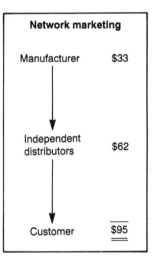

Conventional marketing	
Manufacturer	$33
↓	
Advertising	$14
↓	
Salesforce	$10
↓	
Wholesaler	£10
↓	
Retailer	$33
↓	
Customer	$100

Network marketing	
Manufacturer	$33
↓	
Independent distributors	$62
↓	
Customer	$95

The MANUFACTURER is happy because he has simplified all his middleman costs; and as an even bigger bonus, has replaced his most unreliable cost, advertising, with the word-of-mouth recommendation of independent distributors running their own businesses.

The DISTRIBUTOR is happy because the rewards (and they're not just financial rewards) are potentially far higher than in a traditional marketing setup.

The CUSTOMER is happy because the product is good value, comes recommended by a friend, and can often be tried out at home before buying.

As the group marketing manager of US Sprint put it when it used networking to compete with the telecommunications giant AT&T (a David-and-Goliath trade battle which it won):

Network marketing is the most powerful way yet found of putting the product in front of the consumer.

The modern way

Network marketing is classified as a modern form of direct selling. But the two are hugely different. You might as well compare riding a bike with driving the latest model car. And it's not just the difference between pedal power, where you have to do everything yourself, and a combustion engine which takes you smoothly where you want to go. In direct selling, you are knocking on strangers' doors. Network marketing, by contrast, is a contact business where you get in touch on a friendly basis with people you already know.

So independent distributors are not encouraged to consider themselves salespeople. However, it is helpful to know that most sizable network marketing companies are members of the Direct Selling Association, and have agreed to abide by a strict Code of Ethics which offers comprehensive protection both to new distributors and customers. When you are invited to become part of network marketing, it is worth asking whether the company concerned is a member of the DSA. If so, its system will have been thoroughly vetted.

Network marketing is also one of the few business methods so far discovered where you can only become wealthy by helping others to become wealthy too. It happens through the process of DUPLICATION.

Duplication

You will find the word duplication coming up again and again in network marketing. It is central to the whole business of building a business, and teaching others how to do the same. You duplicate your efforts; you duplicate your teaching methods; and the people you sponsor duplicate what you have taught them to do.

Mathematically, it is known as geometric progression. It has awesome power. If, on the first day of the month, you put a cent in a piggy bank, and the following day 2 cents, and the third day 4 cents, and so on until the end of the month – how much money would you have at the end of 30 days? $1,000? $10,000?

In fact, the answer is: more than $5 million.

And even though in real life nothing turns out to be as perfect as this, the principle of building a network is just as simple. You sponsor two people, those two people sponsor two more, and those four sponsor two each to make eight . . .

It's not very different from a family tree, where a couple get together and form the beginnings of a new lineage. By the time the third or fourth generation has been reached, the number of cousins and in-laws can be 50 or more.

In a rudimentary form, the idea of duplication was first applied to business about 50 years ago. It came about because direct selling has a built-in problem. Suppose a company hires a salesman to open up a new territory. Working maybe 12 hours a day, he begins to do really well. Great, the company thinks – let's put in another salesman, and we'll make twice as many sales.

But how does the first salesman feel about this? Not good. He's had his territory carved up, he's in competition with someone new, sales are harder to make, and he's already working all the hours he can stay awake. So he quits to sell another product for someone else.

Network begins

It seems to have been the US company California Vitamins, in the 1940's, which first found a way of resolving this. It decided to give the salesman a reward if he could generate new business in his territory through bringing in other people to help him. He received a bonus for each new person he recruited, and also a small commission on the increased turnover. Suddenly, the salesman was happy again. Even if he brought in only two new people, and others did the same, this is what happened:

LEADER	1st level	Total 1
X 2		+
——		
2	2nd level	2
X 2		+
——		
4	3rd level	4
X 2		+
——		
8	4th level	8
X 2		+
——		
16	5th level	16
——		——
	Total:	31

California Vitamins could hardly believe their luck. Previously, the salesman on his own had moved product worth, say, $500 a month (remember, it was the 1940s). Now, through encouraging him to duplicate his efforts, they had a turnover of 31 X $500 = $15,500.

But this was only the beginning. People began to realize that if they sponsored just one more person, and taught everyone to do the same, the power of geometric progression would give their group far more strength in numbers.

They didn't even have to work much harder to do it. Instead of starting with two people, they started with three, and taught these three how to sponsor three more, and so on down the line.

But if the difference at the beginning was only one extra new person, look at what happened after five levels:

LEADER	1st level	Total 1
X 3		+
3	2nd level	3
X 3		+
9	3rd level	9
X 3		+
27	4th level	27
X 3		+
81	5th level	81
	Total:	121

Even if the average amount of product moved by each person was lower, at $400, the monthly turnover was now tremendous: nearly $50,000. Yet all the leader had done was find one extra person in the first month, and taught others to do the same.

Growing by word of mouth

Around this time, in the natural course of events, other things happened to network marketing. Firstly the distributors, because of the large numbers needed, stopped being the exclusive preserve of male door-knockers working in their own territory. Instead, it became an army of part-timers looking for some extra income. And because of the nature of California Vitamin's products, these now included many women.

Secondly - and just as important – these women found they were able to earn good money not from selling on the road, as their husbands had been doing, but simply from sharing with friends what California Vitamins had to offer. At coffee mornings all over the west coast of America, women were introduced to California Vitamins, decided they liked it, and began to form networks of their own.

This word-of-mouth recommendation from friend to friend marked the true birth of network marketing. And almost simultaneously, a third thing happened: some people began to get very wealthy indeed.

Finding five

Again, it had to do with the power of numbers. Whereas the full-time salesmen might have had difficulty finding even two good fellow-salesmen prepared to switch jobs, almost everybody has more than two friends who want to make a bit of extra money. It became the goal of the new breed of network marketers to multiply themselves by 5.

Today, that is the norm. Five levels times 5 people is the total you will be encouraged to aim for. And even though the numbers may look extraordinarily large, the law of geometrical progression is so powerful that they happen.

Because all you have done is find five people in the first place, instead of two or three – and taught others to do the same:

LEADER	1st level	Total 1
X 5		+
———		
5	2nd level	5
X 5		+
———		
25	3rd level	25
X 5		+
———		
125	4th level	125
X 5		+
———		
625	5th level	625
———		———
	Total:	781

California Vitamins found, of course, that it took longer for networks to build to this level than the first 2 X 2 format. But so what? At the end of it, if everyone averaged even a $300 product order, monthly turnover was nearly $250,000 – an annual rate approaching $3 million.

Yet all that had happened, to change the network size from 31 to 781, was for the original person to share California Vitamins with five people instead of two – and teach them and their five people to do the same.

As a California Vitamins executive put it to a group of successful women: *Ladies, you have invented a new concept of mathematics. You have proved to me that the difference between 31 and 781 is 3!*

The reward factor

Now, imagine the position of the original salesman, who would probably have left the company if California Vitamins hadn't devised their new reward system.

With a turnover in his group of around $3,000,000 a year, his 2% commission was earning him $60,000. And he wasn't even having to work the 12 hours a day that he used to. He could take holidays – a month, two months – and his group would still turn over almost exactly the same amount, because he was only one of 781.

What's more, people were happy and non-competitive. The normal cutthroat corporate climb to the top had been turned on its head. Look at these two diagrams. On the left is the shape of a typical company, with 625 people at its lowest level of management, all hoping to climb the ladder to become managing director. At each level, there is only one promotion for every five people. Competition between colleagues is fierce and unending.

On the right is how network marketing shapes up. The more people who come in, the better it is for everyone. Instead of competing, you teach how to succeed. The more, the merrier. It is a revolutionary business concept.

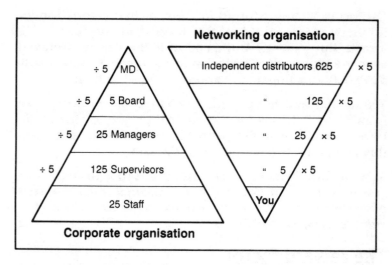

By the end of the 1960s, network marketing had become an established part of the American business system, and was expanding to other countries as well. Everything seemed set fair – until pyramids suddenly got themselves a bad name.

Chapter 4

NETWORKING ETHICS

The pyramid scams lasted only a few years, in the early 1970s, before they were made illegal in the US, the UK, and most countries on the continent of Europe. They were totally different from network marketing, which is designed to provide long-term benefits with the same rules for all. Instead, they were get-rich-if-you-can-and-get-out-quick schemes designed to trick the gullible.

Typically, the promoter would print glossy brochures singing the praises of a new product (in a previous life, he would probably have been a sideshow barker). The product was frequently some variant of snake oil whose market price was impossible to determine. Then, with some associates, he would stage frenzied recruiting meetings where he put about the message that this was an opportunity where nobody could fail – if they signed up *right now*.

The thousands of Americans who did so may have known that they were gambling. Few realized how heavily the odds were rigged against them. Pyramiding is based on simple mathematics: many losers pay a few winners. Just like a chain letter, unless you are in the scheme very near the beginning, you are almost certain to lose your money.

The Direct Selling Association has described them as *illegal scams in which large numbers of people at the bottom of the pyramid pay money to a few people at the top. Each new participant pays for the chance to advance to the top and profit from payments of others who might join later.*

A typical pyramid looks like this:

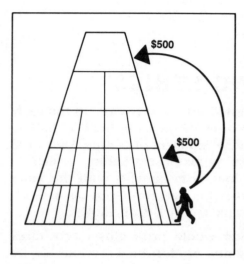

In this example, the promoter at the top would make $16,000, and you would be $1,000 poorer. To reach the top yourself, everyone above you would have to be paid off in full – and a total of 512 new people would have to be recruited. Sooner or later, there are simply not enough willing participants, and the pyramid collapses, leaving you as a loser.

Nearly all pyramid schemes require you to:

- Pay a substantial fee in return for the right to sell product (*a headhunting fee*).
- Purchase a substantial amount of non-returnable product (*inventory loading*).

Pyramids made illegal

A lot of people were taken in. So in the 1970s, various laws were implemented to protect the unsuspecting. Some of the biggest names in pyramiding, such as *Holiday Magic and Dare To Be Great*, were taken to court and convicted.

The decisions hit genuine network marketing companies hard. They were tarred with the same brush as the pyramid scams. The biggest networking company of all, Amway Corporation, was itself accused by the Federal Trade Commission of illegal pyramiding.

In 1979, after a long court battle, Amway won. The judge found that its Marketing Plan (describing how it rewarded its distributors) was significantly different from the condemned pyramid plans. There was no headhunting fee, and no inventory loading; if new distributors decided the business was not for them, and wanted to quit, any unused product would be bought back. Moreover, Amway's emphasis was on retailing. To qualify for overrides, a distributor had to make 10 retail sales per month.

Today, with refinements, this court ruling has become the foundation stone on which reputable network marketing companies rest. The DSA's Code of Ethics (see Appendix) bans pyramiding and false promises of potential earnings. It insists on company buy-back of surplus product. Most countries also prohibit exorbitant entry fees (in the UK, for instance, the maximum is £75 – about $120; in the US, most companies voluntarily charge much less than this). Also, a written contract, with a number of strict conditions, has to exist between the company and the independent distributor.

Above all, there must be genuine product for sale. For as we saw earlier, the purpose of network marketing is to distribute product from manufacturer to customer.

The result in the 1980s was that network marketing began to mushroom. Throughout the difficult years of the pyramid controversy, about 30 companies had kept going. Now they were joined, first by a few dozens, then by hundreds. A common vocabulary emerged:

RECRUIT: find new distributors for your network, and teach them the business.

SPONSOR: the person who introduced you to the program, and is responsible for helping you in the early stages, so long as you put in the effort.

DEALER (or DISTRIBUTOR): An independent contractor salesperson.

SHARE: Show the product to someone, with a view to him or her buying it, and/or becoming a distributor.

UPLINE: Your sponsor, your sponsor's sponsor, and so on all the way up to the company you have joined.

DOWNLINE: Everyone in your group who joined after you.

FRONT LINE: Your first level of downline distributors.

LEG (or LINE): A part of your group that starts with someone personally sponsored by you.

PURCHASE VOLUME (or PV): The total amount of orders put in to the company by you and your group in a given period.

BONUS: Money paid by the company either as a rebate on personal purchases or as an override on your overall PV.

LEVEL (or GENERATION): Just like a family tree. Companies often pay overrides on four or five generations below you. Easier to draw than describe. This is how three levels (of three each) looks:

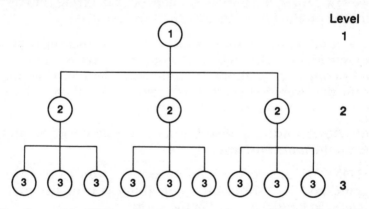

By the mid 1980s the number of network marketing companies in the US had grown from 30 to several hundred (although less than 100 were solid enough to qualify for DSA membership), and newly-signed independent distributors were coming in at the rate of at least one million a year.

The corporate bandwagon

What all these companies cottoned on to was that if they built up a large number of self-motivated, self-replicating independent distributors, and kept them happy by rewarding them for the amount of effort they put in, good products found end-users almost automatically.

The benefits of a networking operation were enormous:

- Low startup costs.
- Rapid expansion and market penetration.
- Little or no expenditure on media advertising; instead, massive exposure by word of mouth.

There was, of course, a huge dropout rate. Thousands of startup businesspeople with a novel product thought they could make a fortune. Usually undercapitalized and unable to handle a distributor network, they vanished almost as fast as they arrived.

The crucial technological development that enabled the best companies to survive and thrive was growth in computer power. Many of the management problems stemmed from the fact that companies simply couldn't keep track of all the transactions and commissions due. Nowadays, every major network marketing company has a dedicated computer system that takes care of this.

In 1993, the Direct Selling Association had 107 members, of whom about two-thirds distributed on a person-to-person basis, and gave bonuses to their distributors according to network marketing principles. Approximately 25 new companies apply each year to join, and about 15 do so after a yearlong screening process. Annually, about 10 drop out. DSA member companies included network marketing subsidiaries of such major corporations as Gillette, Colgate-Palmolive, and Lancaster Colony.

Global growth

And it isn't just an all-American success story.

On the other side of the Pacific, network marketing is thriving. In Japan, where retail premises in big cities cost a fortune, it is an obvious answer. Around 80% of Toyota's domestic sales – which involve a catalogue of products and services as well as cars – are achieved by independent distributors rewarded through the size of their network and turnover.

In Europe, too, it is becoming standard industry practice. Most of the major US networking companies have developed an operation in continental Europe. This is proving highly profitable to many Americans with a US network, and now find that it has spread internationally through the dynamics of internal growth.

Analysis of the record of successful versus unsuccessful businesses shows that a network survives and prospers only if the company offers the distributor three guarantees.

First, the company will abide by an ethical principle:

1. EVERYONE IS ON AN EQUAL FOOTING

Meaning that: no matter when you join, and what place you are in the organization, you have exactly the same opportunities as everyone else.

Cracking the telephone monopoly

One of the most convincing examples of the power of network marketing as applied to big business came with the deregulation of the telecommunications industry in 1989. Two young companies, MCI and US Sprint, decided to attack the near-monopoly held by AT $ T.

In a single year, AT $ T lost 26% market share – and promptly adopted a form of network marketing itself.

Of course, people who have been in the business longest, worked hardest, and have built the biggest networks, are bound to be making more money than you, when you begin.

But the rules make it perfectly possible - and quite usual - for late starters to overtake those who introduced them.

2. THE PRODUCTS ARE GOOD VALUE

Without exception, the track record of every networking company successful in the long term shows that it has a timely product priced to sell. If nobody buys, the network collapses. It's as straightforward as that.

But good value means something else as well: the products should always contain an automatic "repeat" element. That is to say, customers will reorder product as a matter of course. Repeat sales bring a passive income to distributors, so that they go on earning even when they're not working.

3. THE BUSINESS IS SIMPLE

When you are first confronted with a company's marketing plan – its particular way of rewarding its distributors – this may not seem to be so. You will very likely find a ladder of promotion that gives you a complex series of bonuses and percentage commissions depending on how much volume you and your network have achieved.

But virtually all these marketing plans are simple at heart. They offer rewards in three areas:

* RETAILING – you profit from an end-user buying your product.

* WHOLESALING – you profit from supplying your new people with inventory.

* NETWORKING – the company pays you a small percentage on your group's turnover.

If you're just looking for a bit of part-time income, most of your money will come from the first two activities.

But if you want to become a professional network marketer, and plan to build a full-time business, it is invariably the third aspect that generates the huge sums of money that some people are able to make. It is this small percentage, paid on the volume you have helped create through hundreds or thousands of people in your group, which in the end provides not just the six-figure annual profits, but the ability to retire on a passive income.

As John Paul Getty put it: *I would rather earn 1% of 100 people's effort, than 100% of my own.*

Networking millionaires

For many, network marketing has paid off handsomely over the years. Undoubtedly a number of people authentically earn more than $1m annually, and thousands well in excess of $100,000.

But beware anyone who makes bigger claims than this – and particularly, take with a dose of salt a notorious magazine article sometimes quoted when recruiting. It claims that network marketing has created 100,000 $ millionaires in the US.

This is absurd. You should remember that the vast majority of distributors are in the business to make a modest secondary income, and are happy to keep it that way. Just a few high-flyers make it into the stratosphere. However, the exciting thing is that it is still possible for you to join them. Network marketing contains the potential for ordinary people, including yourself and anyone you recruit, to achieve extraordinary earnings (even $1 million a year). And everyone will have started in the same way, with a few good friends and a minimal amount of capital.

Chapter 5

"YOU DON'T HAVE TO SELL..."

At this point, in any study of network marketing, you come face to face with a big puzzle.

Clearly, the aim of the companies is to sell as much product as they possibly can. That's why they're using network marketing. It works. It moves product. It sells.

Yet you, the distributor, are often told: you don't have to sell.

How can this be? What's the answer?

It's an important issue, because at least 95% of us hate every aspect of selling, believe we're no good at selling, and especially dislike the idea of selling to friends.

It's also the main reason why people turn down the opportunity of profiting from network marketing. Most people, when they have been introduced to the opportunity properly, become enthusiastic very quickly.

OK, I appreciate it's not a pyramid.

Yes, it's obviously a fast-growing business.

Sure, I can see how you make money out of it.

Yes, I like the product.

Of course I know people who'd like to be better off.

BUT:

I'm sorry, I'd be hopeless at selling - let alone to my friends.

Which is a pity, because you truly do not have to "sell", in any sense of the word as we normally understand it.

If you want an answer to the puzzle, it lies in the nature of building a network. Look carefully at the section which follows. Network marketing is simple but revolutionary. And it is so different from any other "selling" concept you have come across before that it is bound to take time to sink in.

There are just four essential things you have to do – and keep on doing - if you want to lay down the foundations for a successful network marketing business. Not one of them involves the word "selling".

These are what they are:

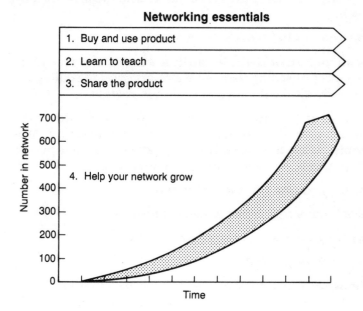

Networking essentials

1. Buy and use product
2. Learn to teach
3. Share the product
4. Help your network grow

Number in network

700
600
500
400
300
200
100
0

Time

Let's look at these essentials in more detail. They are the like the four cylinders in the new car you are driving.

Keep them turning over, and the engine will get you smoothly where you want to go. Stop firing on any of them, and you will eventually stutter to a halt.

1. BUY AND USE SOME PRODUCTS

This is your starting point. By all means look around different network marketing possibilities before you reach for your cheque book, but to get moving there is only one thing to do: buy some products and use them.

If you don't, you won't begin to know what you're dealing with. And unless you like the product line, and have faith in it, you will be unconvincing when it comes to building a network. If you've chosen the right product, you will feel good about using it, and excited about its benefits to others. You will find yourself wanting to describe how well it works. And who will you tell first? Your family and friends, of course.

2. LEARN TO TEACH

Next, your aim is to build a circle of people as enthusiastic and committed as you. There are ways of doing this – and ways of putting people off. The next chapter will give you a few introductory pointers as to which ways work best.

To begin with, talk to your sponsor, and find out as much as possible about the business face to face. Remember that when you in turn share the opportunity with a friend, you will be asked the same questions. So listen to how your sponsor goes about answering them. You will learn the facts that explain your new business properly, and learn how skepticism is overcome – your own included.

Network marketing opens up genuine and unique possibilities for you to develop as a person and to build a sizable business. It is simple in concept but sophisticated in practice. Nobody can expect to understand or appreciate its subtleties on day one. Whether you expect to earn an extra $10,000 a year, or $30,000, or $100,000, you can hardly expect to do it without putting yourself on a learning curve. And in network marketing, that means learning how to teach people to teach other people to do the same as you.

The whole of your first month can be regarded as an intensive training period. Certainly, you should earn as you learn. But if your business is to be long-lasting and successful, you absolutely have to become a teacher yourself. The better the networking company you choose, the more opportunities for training there will be. You should aim to become an even better teacher than the person who introduced you.

3. SHARE THE PRODUCT

This aspect of network marketing – sharing – is the closest you will come to selling. But you will find the two are very different.

"Selling", to most people, means persuading someone to buy something they neither need nor want, and probably can't afford anyway. "Selling", of this sort, is hostile, and unwelcome.

"Sharing", on the other hand, is entirely friendly. You share all sorts of things with friends and family: an experience, an opinion of a film or restaurant, a joke, books, magazines, a power tool, news, gossip, a vacation, bargains, opinions. It's part of civilized life. Sharing is simply day-to-day socializing.

And sharing is at the heart of network marketing. Anybody you talk to who becomes interested in the opportunity will automatically, just like yourself, want to try the product out and use it – without any further encouragement from you. Share it with them. Letthem try it.

A number of companies offer gift introductory packs, or free trial use, of their products. This, too, is another way of sharing and discussing both the product and the business opportunity. If someone likes the product, but for any of a number of reasons doesn'twant to join your network, the chances are that he or she will be a buyer. Excellent. You will have made a retail sale without even trying – by sharing.

Retailing is the key to getting your business started. When people buy product, you make an immediate profit. It's positive cash flow, as your bank manager or any businessperson will tell you. It introduces you to new people who may want to join your network. It provides end-users for the product, without whom the company would go out of business.

But even though you will find retailing gets easier the more you go along, you should still ration the time you spend on it. Because the final essential is:

4. HELP YOUR NETWORK GROW

Different sponsors will give you different guidelines on how you should divide your time between retailing and building your network. One sensible suggestion is that you should reckon, initially, on 40% retailing, 40% sharing the opportunity, and 20% on management and training. As time goes by, and you have a large network to look after, the retailing side may drop to 20% or even 10%.

Because you should always keep your ultimate goals in mind. You are looking towards changing your life. And you can only achieve this through teaching and motivating others to do the same as you. Provided you manage this, your network will grow eventually to such a size that you can achieve a six-figure passive income. Although this may take three to five years, the law of geometric progression will work in your favor in the end.

All this is not to say that people with sales skills – trained or natural – are unwelcome in network marketing. Some become outstandingly successful. But all of them have found that conventional sales techniques are largely irrelevant. Indeed, they can get in the way of progress.

Graphically, it is easy to see what happens if you spend too much time retailing. Your networking income never gets a chance to take off:

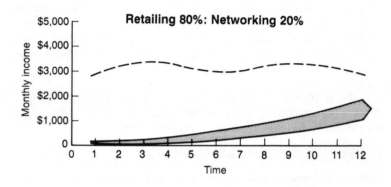

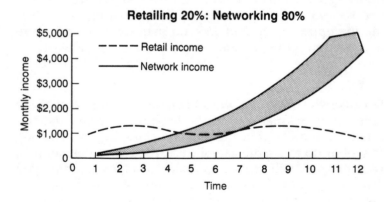

The trouble with salespeople is that this split goes against their instinct and training. Usually, their immediate reaction to the opportunity offered by network marketing is to jump in with both feet and either: (a) sponsor as many people as possible; or (b), sell as much product as possible.

Either way will almost certainly bring headaches, or worse. Let's illustrate this with what happens, typically, to three different sorts of people coming into network marketing for the first time. For simplicity, we'll say they all have jobs bringing in about $3,000 a month, and see how well they do with their different approaches.

Salestype 1

The first person, Salestype 1, decides to sponsor like crazy. In spite of keeping going at her full-time job, she's so dynamic that she sponsors 15 people in her first month, and 15 people in her second month. With this total in her network, she has reached the first management level, and is entitled to good bonuses and commissions on the volume her network achieves.

But what's happened? With 30 people all looking to her to show them what to do next, how much time has she given to each? An hour? An evening? Certainly not more - she's been too busy sponsoring everybody else.

So by the end of the second month, a very large number of the people she sponsored in the first month will have lost interest. They didn't have her ambition and natural sales skills, and because she was the only person they'd met in the business, they didn't knowhow to go about sponsoring in any other way. So they became despondent, and decided network marketing wasn't for them.

By month three, Salestype 1 was running out of friends to sponsor. Being as good as she was, she still managed to find, let's say, 10. But by now she had lost 15 – and the other 15 weren't doing brilliantly either.

In month four, Salestype 1 looked at her bank account and found her income was declining. Her network simply wasn't performing. Impatient for results, she quit, leaving behind her a lot of disappointed people who would never know what an opportunity they had missed – because they hadn't had the guidance or information necessary to start a business.

Salestype 2

Now the story of Salestype 2. He loved the product, and knew exactly how to sell it. In fact, he gave up his existing commission-based sales job to do it. The opportunity seemed so much greater. In a way, he was right. In the first month he made himself $3,000 clear profit. In month two, with bonuses and commissions paid by the company, he had nearly doubled that. By month three, working all the hours he could, he had pushed his profit above $6,000.

But what happened then? His earnings hit a barrier. He couldn't work any more hours. He couldn't squeeze out any more profit. He was making a decent living – but he was doing it all on his own, behaving as if networking was just direct selling under another name.

So he decided to set aside some time to build a network. And what happened? His retail income immediately dropped. He had left his regular job. His monthly earnings were on a rollercoaster – downwards. Providing he could tough it out for a few lean months, the chances were that he would win through in the end. But he had wasted half a year believing his sales skills alone would make him wealthy.

The teacher-type

And lastly the story of the Teacher (not specifically a teacher by profession: just a person able to talk, train, and motivate). She played it by the rules: some retailing, some networking.

Being sensible, she kept her regular job for the time being. She spent 4-6 hours a week retailing, and another 6-8 hours contacting friends, and advising them how best to go about building their own businesses.

The retailing brought in $500-$1,000 a month. The network delivered nothing to begin with, but more and more as time went on. After a few months, income from the two activities added up to more than she was regularly earning. What should she do? Pack in her job and take up network marketing full-time? Carry on with the

---

UNEQUAL OPPORTUNITY?

Terri Gehler, in her fifties and living in Aurora, Colorado, has found a way through network marketing to live a fulfilled life. After finding a company that specialized in nutritional products (a previous interest of hers), she set about building a business part-time.

An educator by background (she has a Ph.D., and was in the principal's office in the Aurora School District), she also devoted time to volunteer work.

When I discovered network marketing, it seemed the ideal solution for me. I wanted to run my own business, and I wanted time in the community. It worked out. I aim to spend 20 hours a week in my business, which gives me more than enough income to live comfortably.

Terri is now active the Aurora Branch of the American Association of University Women, is on the Medical Review Board for Children's Hospital of Denver, and manages a program for the University of Colorado which trains school administrators.

I believe women are natural networkers. More than men, we like picking up the phone and talking to friends. We nurture people as a matter of course. It's in our genes to help and teach. Most of us have more patience than men.I read somewhere that maybe as many as 90% of parttime network distributors are women. That figure doesn't surprise me at all.

job but with a handsome part-time income? It was an enviable choice.

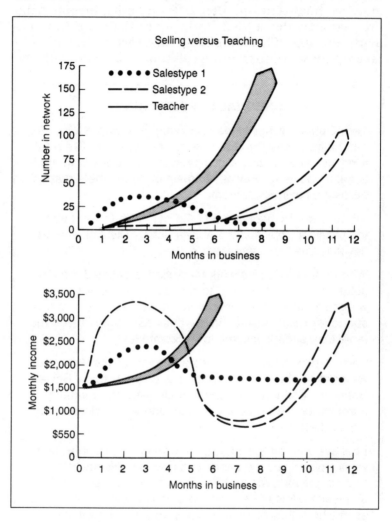

Small wonder that Cheryl Cortese, whose story was told at the beginning of this book, has often said: *Offer my network a salesperson or a teacher and I know who I would choose, every time: the teacher.*

Chapter 6

BUILDING AND TEACHING

So much for the theory and the history. Now for the fun.

Network marketing is extremely sociable. It is all about a lot of people doing a little each. Right now, if you've just been introduced to the concept, and shown the product for the first time, it is almost beyond imagination that in a year's time a hundred, two hundred, perhaps even a thousand people could all be earning themselves money and changing their lives – just because of what you do in the next month.

But that's the way it goes.

All you need do is get started – the right way.

You saw the essentials in the last chapter. The fun comes when you start ringing people up, meeting them, sharing the product and the opportunity – and discovering that some of them become even keener than you.

But who will these people be? How can you possibly build a network of this size when, offhand, you can only think of a handful of people you can go to immediately?

The answer is that you only need a handful of people. Any more is too much, at least to begin with.

Three is ideal; five is the maximum. That's logical. No successful company executive, or officer in the armed forces, ever has more than five key people he is directly supervising – and often it is as few as three. Similarly in network marketing: you must use your time initially to teach just a handful of people to be as successful as you.

Now if you think back to the experience of California Vitamins, you will remember that 1 X 3 X 3 X 3 X 3 will give you a network of 121, and 1 X 5 X 5 X 5 X 5 will give 781. Anywhere in this range is enough to give you a handsome income from the percentage which the company will pay you on your group's turnover.

So all you need do, right away, is to introduce your first three, four, or five. Who do you ring up, and what do you say?

Your sponsor will encourage you to make a large list of everyone you know (statistically, all adults know several hundred people, if only they could remember their names). Next, you will narrow down your list to the 15 or 20 you would most like to work with – andwho are also, in the sponsor's experience, the sort of people most likely to want to succeed in network marketing.

K.I.S.S.

Let's say your first prospect is Jane. You pick up the phone, have a brief hello-and-how-are-you chat with her, and follow it with a short, attention-grabbing invitation. For instance:

> *Jane, I'm starting a new business, and I'm really excited about it. I'd like your opinion. You might be able to help me. Join in, even. Can I come round and talk?*

That's all, believe it or not. The right way of getting started is truly that simple. If Jane says yes, make the earliest possible date - that day, if you like - to go with your sponsor and see her so that, with someone experienced beside you, you can show a video, and share the product and the opportunity. Or you might arrange to pick Jane up and take her to a company briefing.

If you make it more complicated and long-winded, and start giving Jane all sorts of details over the phone, the chances are she'll get the wrong picture. It's impossible to tell the whole story on the phone – so it's best to say as little as possible.

Remember your own reservations when you first heard of network marketing. Didn't you immediately think of

---

AN INVITING PHRASE

Paul Thorne knows what it is like to overcome setbacks. Aged five, he contracted polio, and was not expected to walk again. He was confined to a wheelchair until he was ten, and then moved slowly from braces to crutches to walking, and finally running. At 17, he was junior State track champion, winning the halfmile in 1.58.

After college, where he married Shirley, now his partner in business, he became the youngest Century 21 franchisee, aged 25, and a millionaire. Then, following the 1981 oil collapse, he lost the lot.

In 1986 I had to find something new, and I followed up an advertisement about network marketing. What struck me at once was the possibility of financial freedom, and the opportunity for ordinary people to have extraordinary success.

I really didn't have too much of a problem building a business. But I found many of the people I recruited were telephone shy. At the start, because they were inexperienced, they were tongue tied and couldn't get the message across

So I encourage people to be fairly neutral in what they say to a potential recruit. Often I do it for them, to begin with. I just say: "When can we get together? I'm helping my friend start a new business, and I know he would value your opinion. It's something that you might well want to take a look at yourself."

Pretty well everyone is happy to give an opinion!

pyramid scams, until the difference was explained to you face to face, rather than over the phone? Wasn't one of your first thoughts: *Honestly, I'm not the right person, I wouldn't want to sell to my friends?*

So "KISS" – keep it short and simple. Be exciting for 30 seconds and that's enough. You're only looking for three, four, or five people. You may well have to ring up three times that number to find them – but like everything else in network marketing, the numbers game works in the end.

Creating a network

Let's say – conservatively – that you arrange meetings with 10 people in your first two or three weeks. All you do, with your sponsor, is show and explain. You need never pressure any of your friends to buy or to join.

At each meeting, you will get one of three responses:

1. *It's not for me – but why not try my friends Mary and Jack? They may be interested.*
2. *The product looks good – I'll try it.*
3. *Being a distributor sounds interesting – tell me more.*

Typically, you might get five Response 1's, two Response 2's, and three Response 3's.

So without trying at all hard, and without "selling", you will have done what both you and the company wants: moved its product to some new end-users, and started a new network.

(Responses 2 and 3 both mean sales, because a new distributor will need some product to start doing business).

From just 10 meetings you have set up, your network will begin to form something like this:

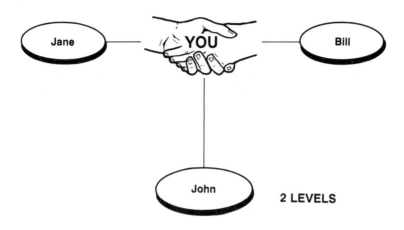

To go on to the next level in your network, you contact more people.

This time, you may not know some of them. The seven friends you saw in stage one who weren't interested, or bought the product, will have given you some names of their own friends who might want to be offered the opportunity as well.

For the time being, you are looking for only two more people to join your network at the 2nd level, to give you your handful of five.

Because additionally, you now have three new distributors in your network who are going to do exactly the same as you: meet 10 people. You will be spending time showing them how to do it – teaching them, just as your sponsor helped you with your first calls, and going along with them.

If they get more or less the same results as you – which they should do if you have sponsored people as keen as you are – they too will sponsor two or three people each, and make a few retail sales.

Your network will begin to look something like this:

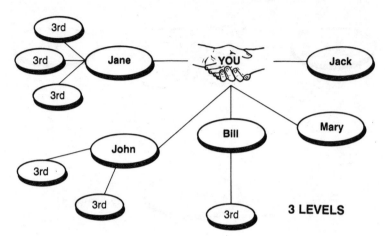

By now, at the end of, say, the second month, you have a full hand. Mary and Jack both joined, so you have enough 2nd level people, and for the moment, you do not want to create any more legs. Your time will be spent mostly on teaching others to do the same as you, with some retailing on the side.

Now you want to create depth in your network, so that it has stability, and allow you to profit through many generations downline from you. With 11 people, you will have made a good start. The network will already have a life of its own. What shape it takes will depend on the quality of the 5 people you have put in the frontline, and on the teaching example you are able to set. You must train, encourage, and motivate. Phone everyone in your group. Go with them to their new people. Take them to training sessions, and let them learn.

Two things are sure:

1. Your network won't develop evenly and regularly as per the 5 times mathematical model.

2. At the same time the power of numbers will win out in the end.

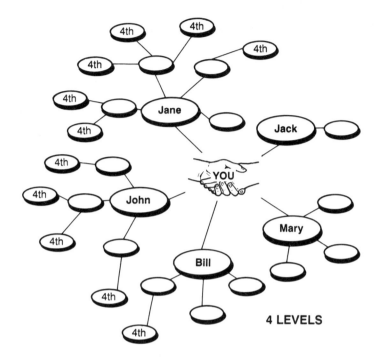

Typically, after a few weeks or a few months, you could have a network that looks something like this. Notice how unevenly it has developed. Jane is leading the field, with a network of 10, plus herself. John has seven, Bill four, Mary three, and Jack one.

This is the way it usually happens. You will find that one of your legs develops startlingly fast. Another may never get off the ground. In another, an unexpected star performer may emerge – someone who is going to earn even more money than you. (Cross your fingers that this will happen: a handful of people like that, and you will be very wealthy).

But the 31 you now have in your network (including yourself) is a large enough number for most companies to promote you to the first level of management, and put you in line for substantial bonuses.

Even more important, your network is now at the point of lift-off. It isn't the number 31 that has brought this about. Salestype 1, whose story was told in the previous chapter, sponsored 30 people in a few weeks – and her network still collapsed a little while later. It's because, with some of your legs, you have gone four deep.

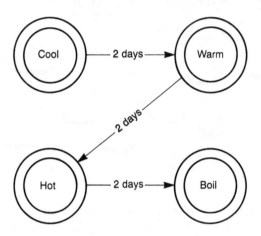

THE FOUR-RING HOTPLATE

One almost sure way of blowing out a good prospect is to try to explain everything at once. It has the same effect as putting a glass of cold water directly on to the boiling plate of a cooker.

Take it gently, but keep the momentum going. "Cool" is the first short telephone call. "Warm" is a visit lasting half an hour or so while you watch a video and show the product. "Hot" is when you introduce them to other people doing well in the business, for instance at a company briefing. "Boiling" is when you have a session setting goals, and make the initial product order.

Let your prospect read this book anywhere between cool and boiling.

Four deep

This is perhaps the most important practical lesson you will have to learn if you are to be successful in network marketing.

Until you have built a leg four deep, it isn't truly self-replicating.

Let's think about the first person you sponsored: Jane. By bringing her into the business, it looks at first glance as though you have duplicated yourself –

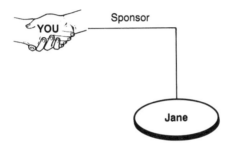

But you haven't – because Jane knows almost nothing yet about practicalities and techniques of building a business of her own. So you go one stage better: you teach Jane that to have her own network, she needs to sponsor people herself. Jane promptly rings up her close friend Tom, who thinks it's a great idea, and signs a registration form.

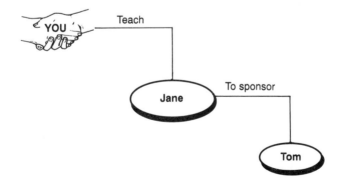

Deceptively, this looks better, as though you and Jane are now on your way. But it is still not self-perpetuating. Because the only thing Tom knows about the business is what Jane showed him – that he has to sponsor other close friends. Let's say he makes a few unsatisfactory phone calls and gets no results. What happens? He gives up. Your line stops right there. Then Jane, too, becomes disheartened. Now your leg is producing no results at all.

To prevent this happening, you have to teach *the right teaching attitudes at the very beginning*.

You don't just teach Jane to sponsor Tom, you teach Jane how to teach Tom to sponsor someone else.

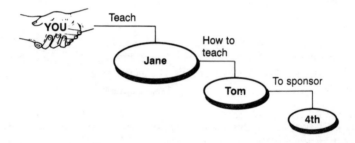

This is where the effort and skills in network building take place: at the very beginning. You will be patiently spending time with Jane, establishing her goals, working through her list of prospects, phoning and visiting her new people, and taking her and them to training meetings.

Jane will copy what you do – be sure of that. She'll have the reassurance of someone experienced by her side in the early stages, and she'll pass this habit on. It will duplicate itself down Jane's line, 10 or 15 deep.

You will have put yourself in a position where, at levels far beyond your direct control, your network will grow and thrive entirely of its own accord. Once you have done this you are secure. You can go away on holiday –

or better still, go and create another leg- safe in the knowledge that this part of your network now has a built-in dynamic for growth.

Network growth

How far and how fast your network grows will depend on:

- How soon you find three, four, or five good people. It can take days – or months. You may well have to contact several times the eventual number. But they're around. You just have to keep at it.
- How many hours a week you're prepared to spend teaching them, and going to meetings with them - and doing the same with the first new level of people they introduce.

After a solid year in the business - providing you remember to teach how to teach – you will probably find 100 – 600 in your network. Those who consistently teach the right habits can always reach the 100 plus level – and from then on, the sky is the limit.

Whatever the figure, your network will grow so long as you remember to build four deep:

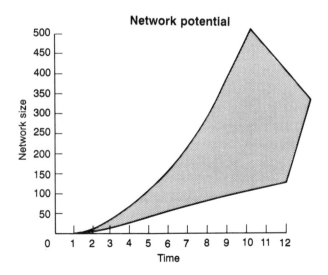

SATURATION

If you take geometric progression to its logical conclusion, it raises a question which deserves answering:

Network marketing is obviously booming – so what's going to happen when it saturates? Surely everyone will be in on it soon, and there'll be nowhere for me to go?

The general point of comfort here is that although, numerically, if you multiply 5 X 5 a few times (12 times, in fact), you run out of adult population in the US, the reality is that human nature stops it happening. Most people are fundamentally too idle to benefit from network marketing, except by buying product.

In the US at the end of 1993, perhaps 3.5 million out of an adult population of about 250 million were to some degree active in the networking business: hardly more than 1%. That leaves nearly 99% of people as potential buyers, or recruits.

Moreover, Americans change jobs on average every 3.7 years, a mobility which constantly refreshes the pool of network marketing distributors.

In any field of commerce, saturation is a practical impossibility. Surely nearly all US homes have a refrigerator? Well yes. But 1992 was the best year for refrigerator sales in history.

Amway Corporation has led the field in network marketing for 34 years – ample time to saturate, if it were ever going to happen. But Amway is still expanding. Its sales grew in 1992 to $4 billion, an increase during the year of $1 billion.

Chapter 7

IS IT FOR YOU?

There's another thing you have to teach.

You have to teach people to dream.

Barbara Rebold is good at that. Brought up in Cincinatti, Ohio, she joined network marketing in 1987, when she was 34 years old and running her own small advertising company. Six years on, having sold her business, she was one of the top earners in the networking company she chose, with an organization numbering thousands.

I got there because I dreamed – and turned my dreams into goals, she says.

One of her dreams had a heartwarming conclusion: *I was one of a family of nine, with five sisters and three brothers. My parents weren't well off, so we never had the money for us all to go on vacation together. Even as a child, I dreamed how wonderful this would be.*

So when I came into network marketing, and my sponsor told me to write down goals that I wanted to achieve, I put this down as one of them.

December, 1993, was my fortieth birthday. By that time I was living in Florida – another of my goals. I celebrated by inviting every member of my family for a week's non-stop party in Orlando. Network marketing enabled me to pick up the tab for the whole reunion – air fares, hotels, Disneyland, the lot. And it wasn't just my eight brothers and sisters. By then, with children and all, the number had risen to 23!

BARBARA'S ORIGINAL 1987 GOALS

1. Own a home in Florida
2. Be debt free except for home mortgage
3. Learn to speak in front of 200 people
4. Travel to Europe
5. Support a children's Foundation
6. Learn to snow ski
7. Complete the New York City marathon
8. Take the whole family on vacation to Disney World
9 A long-lasting, healthy relationship
10. In-home fitness center
11. $150,000 in the bank
12. Drive and walk over a bridge
13. Hike the Smokey Mountains
14. $200,000 annual income
15. Physically fit until the day I die

Six years later, she had attained all her goals (except the last, which is a lifelong process.)

In network marketing, you are encouraged to dream your wildest dreams, and turn these into goals that you picture in your mind. Then you draw up a realistic action plan so that you can attain them within a timescale which you set yourself.

Barbara Rebold explains: *You write down a series of mini-goals and deadlines, so that you have something to aim for on the way, and know how many hours you have to work to make them happen.*

In broad outline, her mini-goals were simple. Within six months, she would have at least 30 people in her network; within a year, 100; within 18 months, 300; within two years, 1,000. These were promises to herself, and she wouldn't break them, no matter what. She wrote down in detail her plan of how many people she would need to contact, week by week and day by day.

There is a strangely under-publicised branch of science (see Box) which shows that the human mind has an extraordinary capacity, working well below the level of consciousness, to direct us to our goals – providing our desire to achieve these goals is strong enough, and we keep reminding ourselves what they are. Academic research has shown that 95% of people never set goals for themselves. The 5% who do – and better still, those who write down their goals and refer to them daily – achieve results far and away better than the rest. Of course, Barbara's dreams were different from yours. And what might those be? To stop working? Buy a better house? Move to another area? Spend more time with your family? Do something about the way your parents live? Put your children in a good school?

Whatever your personal desire, one of the first things you will be taught when you come into the business is: write down your goals. Barbara Rebold says emphatically:

CYBERNETICS

In the 1940s, scientists working at the Massachusetts Institute of Technology coined a new word, cybernetics, to describe the work they were doing on sophisticated, self-correcting guidance systems for missiles. The word comes from the Greek for "helmsman".

All animals – humans particularly – are biological cybernetic systems, far more advanced than any computer system yet developed. Throughout their lives, they are capable of learning from mistakes, and use a natural process of feedback to steer them to their target - like a baby determined to learn to walk.

But they can only do this if they know precisely what the target, or "goal", is. Ill-defined goals bring erratic helmsmanship. By contrast, the human mind will chart its way infallibly to a goal which is clear and focused, taking the best route possible in changing circumstances.

GOALS ARE AS ESSENTIAL TO SUCCESS

AS AIR IS TO LIFE.

The second thing you will be taught also has a psychological basis. It sounds tough, but will surely happen if you take your new network marketing business seriously: *Be prepared to change.*

Changing from within

The first thing you must develop is determination. Barbara, deep down inside, made up her mind that, more than anything else in the world, she wanted to get out of her rut. Instead of watching TV, she spent her evenings and weekends on the phone, or visiting people, or going to meetings.

And because she was so determined, and was contacting and teaching so many new people, quite quickly she found herself growing in self-belief. The more dedicated she was, the more confident she became. And finally there she was in the fall of 1993, all her goals achieved except number 8, standing at the airport in Orlando, waiting for her family to step off the plane.

She tells new people coming into the business: *If you want your life to change – your financial status, your enjoyment, your confidence – don't expect a free ride. In network marketing, you're aboard a vehicle that can transform your life. But to get where you want, come of your comfort zone and behave more positively than you ever have before.*

Most people make the mistake, initially, of underestimating the power of network marketing. Understandably, they lack belief – until they have been to enough meetings, and had the chance of talking to people who have revolutionized the way they live.

But the fact is that network marketing is an extremely sophisticated distribution system which swiftly and effectively moves product from factory to end-user. Because it is so simple in concept, so easy for people to join, and so flexible in the way it provides additional income, nobody can be blamed for first thinking, *this seems too good to be true.*

The alternatives

But what are the alternatives, if you want to earn some extra money, or start a business of your own? Compare it with any other type of commercial opportunity currently being advertised. Most of these involve telephone selling, or badly-paid hourly rates for repetitive work – which in any event would mean working for somebody else, rather than yourself.

As another way of making money from home, you could market whatever skills you happen to have – decorating, or sewing, or baby care, or cooking, or cleaning, or handicrafts, or consultancy. Here two problems crop up: you have to find a way of letting people knowyou are available (advertising, mail-shots, etc.); and you are limited by the fact that there are only 24 hours in a day, of whichyou have to sleep for at least six. And how much an hour can you charge? $15? $20? $30? The retail prospects, alone, from network marketing are probably better.

Franchising

Let's look at the franchising option again. Statistics show that if you put together the money to buy one, you are better than 90% likely to succeed in some degree. And if you want to go into business on your own for the first time, any worthwhile franchiser will insist you undergo training to help make your business successful. You will have a protected territory, where you may be competing against similar businesses, but will have exclusivity on the name of the company you have chosen.

Compared with network marketing, the variety of businesses is much larger. If you get hold of a copy of the official guide published by the International Franchise

Association in Washington, DC, you will find a list of more than 5,000 franchises on offer.

Restaurants, take-outs, retail shops, and hotels make up three-quarter of business format franchise sales, and none of these is suitable for network marketing. All the go-it-alone opportunities suggested on the previous page, and many more, are available in franchised form. You will have the advantages of the experience of the franchiser, cheaper inventory through central buying, and you should get some advertising support.

Those are some of the pluses. On the other side of the coin, the phrase *you're in business for yourself, but not by yourself* means that you are not truly your own boss. You will have to conform to the franchiser's system, and are likely to have little creative business freedom, except in certain areas of marketing. It is a halfway house between being employed and being genuinely independent. At the same time you will be responsible for the headaches which go with hiring and firing employees.

Then there is the risk if you happen to be among the unfortunate few who fail. You could lose your savings, and possibly the house you have put up as security against the money you have borrowed.

Lastly, your rewards are finite. Franchisers are prohibited by law from giving earnings expectations. You can make an estimate yourself by talking to other franchisees. But as a general rule, do not expect to do better than break even in your first year *without paying yourself* (which is why the cost of a $15,000 franchise rises to $50,000 after providing for working capital). After your business is successfully established, you may find yourself gaining a pretax return of perhaps 20–40% a year on your investment. But that will be that. A single store with a fixed amount of shelf space can only generate a certain volume of retail sales. If you want to expand, you will have to buy another franchise.

Head office backup

There are some similarities in all this with network marketing, but not many. (The most obvious one is that the more hours you put in, the more likely you are to succeed.) So far as backup is concerned, the networking company, if it is a good one, will handle some of the elements which make startup businesses vulnerable, including:

* Product development

* Financing costs of manufacture and stock

* Administration costs of supplying distributors

* Costs of administering network payroll

* Handling of regulatory bodies

As for control over your activities, you will probably be restricted to use of company literature and promotional tools (to prevent you making false claims about the products or the business potential). But to a great extent, you are genuinely independent, and free to go your own way.

Training

As with franchising, there will be training - though less formally. You know now from the nature of the business that your sponsor will only benefit if you benefit, so that means passing on all the experience that she or he has. Additionally, you are likely to find local meetings laid on by experienced senior distributors in your area, telephone conference calls, and large-scale regional meetings arranged by the company (see Box).

So the phrase is true of both kinds of marketing: *you are in business for yourself, but not by yourself.* But after that, franchising and networking part company.

Startup investment. Usually $25 – $75. After that you will be encouraged to make a modest initial investment (perhaps $100) in "tools of the trade" – sales aids, attendance at training meetings. If you want to buy inventory costing, say, $1,500, most companies have credit arrangements, if you need them.

Overheads. Running costs are minimal: probably an increased phone bill, and some additional gas for your car. You don't have employees, you don't have to pay rent.

Business experience. The sheer range of people making money out of network marketing shows that you don't need special skills. There are ex-truckdrivers with new BMWs, and plenty of parents putting their children through college. Background, education, age, sex, color – it simply doesn't matter who you are or where you come from. The most important skills to develop – and we all have them in us – are being able to talk to people, to explain, and to motivate. Since, to begin with, you will be doing this just to friends and colleagues, it's within your grasp.

MASS MEETINGS

In terms of audience size, some of the meetings are astonishing – indeed, unbelievable to many of my friends in the conventional corporate world. 12,000 people in the Convention Center in Memphis all enjoying themselves? *Don't kid me, there's a sting here somewhere.* 4,000 people in Frankfurt all looking to distribute an American product? *You must be joking.*

Clemens Hergeth, at the age of 32, reached the top distributor level in his networking company within a year, working out of his home in Dusseldorf, Germany.

I was with two major international companies before this. I laid on sales conferences. After lunch, typically, thirty per cent didn't come back. In networking, you can have 3,000 before lunch, and 4,000 afterwards. They've rung up their friends because they're so excited. Amazing!

Territory and potential. The opposite of franchising. Your territory is any country in the world where your company operates. Anyone with a sizable network will tell you that it has expanded of its own accord internationally, and that they receive company checks in currencies from countries they have never visited. As for potential, it is theoretically unlimited. A soundly based network generates momentum of its own.

Risk. In financial terms, minimal. Providing the company is a member of the Direct Selling Association, it will give an undertaking to buy back unused stock at 90% of the purchase price (see Appendix). So if you change your mind about the product or the company or the system after a month, and just pack the whole thing in, you will have wasted your time, and perhaps $250.

Deep end. Another aspect of risk is whether you have to commit yourself and your family to a complete change of career. In network marketing, you don't need to plunge into the deep end – that is, go full-time immediately – to find out if you are going to succeed. The vast majority of distributors start part-time and remain part-time. They're happy with the extra income: in round figures, anything from $250 to $2,500 a month.

You should only go full-time when you have proved to yourself that the business suits you. Then you can start building seriously, and become excited at the thought of $50,000 to $500,000 a year.

Downside?

As with any startup business, there is a downside to network marketing. Even part-time, there are penalties to being your own boss. The hours can be unsociable – if you have a full-time day job, you will have to work in the evenings, and at weekends.

And you will have to be resilient. Many of the people you try to recruit (even the mostly likely prospects) will say no, and some of those you recruit will drop out, because they are not as committed as you. You will have to develop a thick skin, and learn that being rejected is not a personal matter.

So although you can make decent extra money from the day you receive your first delivery of product, it will be six months to a year or more before your network is substantial.

Commitment

In fact, a year's commitment to the business is the minimum period you should have in mind. Anything shorter than 12 months is not enough to even out the ups and downs that the whims of human nature will bring to your network.

Given this length of time, the sheer power of geometric progression usually wins through. Most people quit network marketing in the first few months, when things seem to be going too slowly. So long as you keep on recruiting and retailing, networking is as simple as a two (or five) times table. The only thing is: simple doesn't mean easy.

But the basic concept of network marketing is so sound that it deserves to be repeated:

> YOU CAN MAKE A LIVING MARKETING A
> PRODUCT. BUT YOU CAN MAKE A FORTUNE
> BY BUILDING A NETWORK AND TEACHING
> OTHERS TO DO THE SAME.

Chapter 8

ENVIRONMENTAL COMPANIES

So how to begin choosing a company?

Unless you're a gambler, there seem to me three prime considerations. The company must:

- Be financially sound.
- Have a record of growth and plans for future growth.
- Do business of a sort you enjoy.

The first two are necessary, objective, and can be established through your own research and through taking professional advice.

The third is subjective but crucial. Only you can give the answer. It is even more important than the financial bottom line – because your business won't succeed long-term unless you're comfortable with what you're doing.

However good the company, and the opportunity it offers, you have to sense the need for the product line or service it offers. It is a gut reaction. You must be able to say confidently: *Yes – I'd be happy talking to my friends about this*. If you can't say that, what's the point of being your own boss?

Which brings me back to the reason I wrote this book. I believe that our environment and our health are perceptibly worsening. I believe that as consumers we will spend billions of dollars trying to stave off the damage. I don't see why we shouldn't have a share of those dollars if we're prepared to work for them.

There are three primary concerns in most people's minds – the first two universal, the third a central part of American culture.

WE ALL BREATHE AIR – BUT WE WORRY ABOUT
WHAT IT'S DOING TO OUR LUNGS

WE ALL DRINK WATER – AND WE WORRY
ABOUT ITS QUALITY AND TASTE.

MOST OF US EAT CONVENIENCE FOOD – AND
WE KNOW IT'S NOT DOING US MUCH GOOD.

Air. Water. Nutrition. Those are things people suspect, rightly or wrongly, to be polluted - and the things they can do something about wherever they live or work, and make money out of, too. So I began a trawl through the franchising and networking companies to find which were committed to easing the situation. These would be the companies, I suspected, which would show recent growth, and which would become boom businesses in the 90s.

FRANCHISING

The first surprise, looking at the franchising opportunities, was just how few suitable candidates there were. The 5,000+ members of the International Franchise Association are dominated by the take-outs and fast food restaurants which some would say simply contribute to the problem, rather than solve it.

Air

In the franchising catalogue, there is a category called Environmental Services with just two entries. One of them, Environmental Biotech Inc., is based in Sarasota, Fl. It has the slogan *Environmental Solutions = PROFITS*, which fits neatly with my own philosophy. It describes its business as *utilizing biotechnology and environmen-*

tally safe chemicals for remediation. A franchise needs a minimum investment of around $100,000, and the company has developed 55 outlets since 1991.

Under another heading, there is a company called Environmental Air Services, Inc., in Waco, TX. Its slogan is *Breathe Cleaner Healthier Indoor Air*, and its business is described as *internal air quality assessment and mitigation, air conveyance system decontamination, air washing, filters, fire restoration.* Again, the finance required is around $100,000, and again it shows recent growth: 25 franchised outlets since 1993.

Water

Water conditioning has just two entries, of which the biggest is Culligan International, in Northbrook, IL., in the franchise business since 1939. It is listed as having 749 franchised outlets, requiring investment of up to $150,000. You would benefit from its widely-known brand name (95% of all Americans recognize it). Having profited from the boom in bottled water sales, it now additionally offers a full line of water treatment products to homes and offices.

A less expensive option is Rainsoft Water Conditioning Co., in Elk Grove, IL., where investment can be less than $50,000. Its business is water purification and softening, and it has developed 243 outlets since 1953.

Nutrition

In the category Vitamin and Mineral Stores, there are only two entries, although I came across a related, but unlisted franchising operation which has niche potential. This is Juice Club, Inc., a health food store concept developed in San Luis Obispo, Calif. Freshly-squeezed juices, healthy snacks, and "smoothies" (nutritious blended drinks that substitute for meals) are its main lines.

The company's president, Kirk Perron, says: *We are helping people improve the quality of their lives through nutrition.* In 1993 Juice Club had only three locations, generating $2 million in sales, but there are plans for expansion. Opening a franchise will cost around $200,000.

Of the entries listed in the catalogue, the smaller is Great Earth Vitamin Stores, in West Hollywood, Calif., with 112 outlets developed since 1973. An investment of $100,000+ will be needed.

The household name in this area, however, is GNC - General Nutrition Centers, Pittsburgh, PA, whose slogan is *Where America Shops for Health*. It has nearly 1,000 company owned stores, and nearly 500 franchised outlets.

Market leader

Because it is overwhelmingly a market leader, and has a track record of success that has lasted almost 60 years, I thought it the most appropriate franchising opportunity to examine in some detail. One of the company's leaflets mirrors my own beliefs:

We are experiencing a metamorphosis - when people of all ages and all places demand control over their bodies, their minds, and their health. Research indicates that consumers now want to participate in preventing and managing their health problems, rather than relying totally on their personal physician.

They actively strive to feel better and perform at their optimum level. They seek information about the maintenance of health, physical and mental fitness, nutrition, and vitamins. Approximately 70% of consumers are interested in the nutritional content and quality of food. Increasing numbers are concerned about health hazards, salt, and sugar.

This new self-care movement will continue to grow. By the mid 1990s, the market will generate approximately $3 billion. Higher percentages of the population show a potential for increasing the level of their self-care *health enhancement and, in turn, expenditures.*

In the 10 years 1984-1993 GNC's sales increased 350% from $472 million to $1,682 million. The company offers an assortment of more than 2,800 approved products, the core categories being vitamin and mineral dietary supplements, sport nutrition supplements, healthy food and snack products, naturally-based cosmetics, weight loss products and comfort items.

To qualify as a GNC franchisee, you have to demonstrate a strong personal interest in health and nutrition. You have to be good financial health, too, with $50,000 in available cash, and a net worth of at least $100,000. You can expect the average total investment to be around $150,000. GNC breaks down the low-high figures as:

	Low ($s)	High ($s)
Initial franchise fee	20,000	20,000
Opening inventory	25,000	50,000
Furniture and fixtures, signs	18,000	34,500
Leasehold improvements	10,000	100,000
Deposits, rent, working capital	5,000	10,000
Total franchise package	78,000	214,500

As I wrote earlier, franchisers are not allowed by law to make claims for possible earnings by franchisees. The published average annual sales figure for 942 GNC company operated stores in 1992/93 was a little over $400,000. After deducting cost of goods sold, the gross profit was almost exactly $225,000. Salaries, occupancy costs, and operating expenses brought the net profit per company-operated store to $107,000. If you, as a franchisee, came somewhere close to this average figure, you would then have to deduct further costs – e.g. a royalty percentage on turnover, advertising, accounting, and insurance – before arriving at your personal pretax profit.

NETWORK MARKETING

Network marketing is in a different ballpark. The Direct Selling Association has just over 100 companies as members, of whom three – Amway, Avon, and Mary Kay – have annual sales in excess of $1 billion, and two – Home Interiors and Gifts, and Time-Life – more than £0.5 billion. At the other end of the scale, 80 have sales of less than £100 million.

What is striking about the remainder ($100–500 million), particularly those using some form of network marketing, is the high proportion which include environmental products in their catalogues. Their total is almost the same as in the entire 5,000 franchising operations.

Here, to the best of my knowledge and in alphabetical order, is a complete list of companies in the $100m+ sales bracket which use person-to-person sales techniques, with asterisks to mark whether they have products directed at ongoing problems created by air, water, and nutrition. The date when each started direct selling is also included.

Air	Water	Nutr.	Company
			Electrolux (1924)
			Encyclopaedia Britannica (1920)
	*	*	Herbalife (1980)
			Kirby Company (1914)
		*	Matol Botanical (1984)
		*	Melaleuca (1985)

*	*		Nature's Sunshine Products (1974)
*	*	*	NSA (1970)
		*	Nu Skin (1984)
	*		Regal (1984)
			Rexair/Rainbow (1984)
	*	*	Shaklee (1956)
			Tupperware (1951)
			West Bend (1927)
			Wholesale Warehousing (1985)
			World Book (1917)

Of the 17 companies here, no fewer than seven address themselves to environmental health concerns. To them we can add the giant Amway Corporation (1959), with asterisks for water and nutrition.

Conundrum

There are, of course, far more network marketing companies than this, many of them in the environmental area. The reason I have chosen those with a $100+ million sales base, and with a track record going back for at least ten years, is because it is likely to be a long-lasting company through which you can look forward to a long-term independent business.

But there is a possible downside here. Saturation of a market is impossible, as we saw earlier. But a kind of verbal saturation creeps in. Most adult Americans have been approached half a dozen times to become a network distributor, and it stands to reason that the more famous the name, the more likely they are to have turned the opportunity down already. (This doesn't, by the way, mean that the seventh approach will be unsuccessful: people's circumstances change).

Also, there is a question that many will ask:

Network marketing seems brilliant for those who got in early – but what about us late starters?

The short answer is that network marketing is played on a level playing field. If you complete enough circuits of the running track, you can catch up or overtake those who started before you, but are now easing up because their business has gone so well.

However, if you look at statistics about networking's high-fliers – the people in the six or seven-figure annual income bracket – you will find that the majority of them seem to have come into the company at a time when it was rapidly expanding – close to its inception, or after it had produced a fast-selling new product line. After that comes a period of consolidation, when people taking the route to the top become fewer, and the journey usually takes longer.

Part-time solution

So a more comprehensive answer might be this. *If you're looking for a secondary income, something in the five-figure bracket, the long-standing companies are the safest.* (Terri Gehler's story on page 43 is typical: she works part-time with Shaklee products). *If you're looking for a fortune, you can join the same company, start part-time, and go full-time when you're comfortable. There's still plenty of room at the top for anyone who works hard enough, although it may take three to five years.*

Of the long-established companies, Amway Corporation and Shaklee are the foremost names, and each has two environmental asterisks in the list above. Amway is so well-known and so far ahead of the field in sales volume that it hardly needs an introduction. It first achieved $1+ billion annual sales in 1981, increasing these to $4+ billion in 1993. Its business is conducted in 50+ countries, conducted from headquarters in Ada, Mich., where the complete manufacturing process of the majority of Amway's products is controlled.

Its involvement with environmental concerns is not in doubt. In 1989, the UN presented it with an Environmental Achievement Award in recognition of Amway's "commitment to the cause of environmental protection and awareness, and for its support and encouragement to young people to make the environment a priority concern."

Amway's own mission statement on the subject is that:

The proper use and management of the world's limited resources and the environment are the responsibility of industry and individuals alike. As a leading manufacturer of consumer goods with a direct sales network of more than one million independent distributors worldwide, Amway recognizes its responsibility and role in both fostering and prompting sound environmental stewardship.

Its core business consists of good-value, biodegradable household cleaning products. Aerosols contain no chlorofluorocarbons (which are a cause, it is thought, of damage to the ozone layer).

Its catalogue, now huge, contains a range of "low-ticket" (below $25) and "high-ticket" (above $100) items. (It stands to reason, but is worth saying, that to make a good income you need to distribute a lot of the first compared with fewer of the second.) In-home water treatment systems are included. As for health and fitness, there are vitamin supplements, a weight control system, and exercise equipment.

I talked to a few of the 1 million+ Amway distributors, (including some who had dropped out) to see what they liked and disliked about their work. All of them loved the products, and the concept of network marketing, which conforms closely to the central portion of this book. They liked the element of repeatability built into the Amway product line – a very high proportion of consumers reorder household cleaners.

The most common complaint was the amount of time that had to be spent on paperwork, in order to conform with Amway's highly-regulated system (the most common excuse for dropping out). Some distributors also felt that because Amway's activities were now so widespread, it was to some extent a "buyer's club". That is, compared with earlier days, more product was being consumed within the existing network than was being retailed to new consumers outside it.

But the message I got was on the whole positive. People were pleased with the extra income they were earning (fairly modest, for most of them), and a number were enthusiastically looking forward to going full-time and reaching a higher position in the company.

Shaklee

Shaklee Corporation has a lot going for it, too. Owned since 1989 by the Japanese company Yamanouchi Pharmaceutical Co. Ltd., it has stuck to the original philosophy of its founder, Dr. Forrest C. Shaklee, Sr., in 1956.

> *The health of the environment is intertwined with the health of every person who inherits it. Every product we develop must be respectful of humankind and the Earth, and in harmony with nature and good health . . . a healthy life is one that is filled with happiness and security.*

Like Amway, it received recognition when in 1990, *Family Circle* magazine gave the company a "Green Chip" award for being one of the nation's ten most environmentally conscious companies. Over the years, it has invested more than $80 million in research and development, including rigorous independent clinical studies.

This commitment to the scientific method distances Shaklee from some of the networking companies whose nutritional products owe significantly to ingredients of unproven merit. More than 60,000 quality tests (not involving animals) are conducted by Shaklee each year. As a company spokesperson put it:

> *We spend millions on research. Shaklee products are based on clear scientific evidence rather than the fad of the moment. Our long experience and technical advantages enable us to formulate supplements that are nutritionally balanced with appropriate potency levels for maximum safety and effectiveness. The stakes are high. Poor nutrition has been linked to six out of ten of the leading causes of death. Typically American diets are out of balance. We eat far too much fat, too little fiber, too few complex carbohydrates, too little of foods that contain many essential vitamins and minerals.*

In addition to nutritional products, Shaklee has a large range of phosphate-free biodegradable household cleaners. In water treatment, its BestWater MTS© range contains effective chemical-removal carbon filtration systems, rated a best buy in *Consumer Digest*. Its extensive catalogue also offers home and garden, household care, and personal care products.

If you're looking for a supplemental income through sharing products with neighbors, I rate Shaklee highly. A number of Shaklee distributors make six-figure incomes, and their leading distributors more than $1m per year. It has a reputation for being a friendly and unpressurizing company, and its scientific validity is beyond dispute.

But what about the young, thrusting, would-be entrepreneur who says: *I've enough money to carry me through the first few months. I don't see myself gossiping to housewives. I don't want to wait to get rich, I want to build a business fast, show me an opportunity right now.* What is your answer to that?

There are two: Be a gambler. Or find a good company that is still growing fast, and offers a timely opportunity.

Chapter 9

GROUNDFLOOR OPPORTUNITIES

Sooner or later, whether you're already a network distributor or not, you're likely to be approached by someone offering you a groundfloor opportunity. You'll be told: Get in quick. Don't miss it. This is the big one.

There are probably a couple of hundred network marketing companies (or pseudo-networking) in the US, lurking in the wings outside the main stage of the Direct Selling Association. If they offer you groundfloor opportunities, by definition they won't have two or more years of annual sales figures to present (the length of time any cautious advisor would suggest). But network marketing is such a powerful process that in all likelihood some of them will succeed – and you may indeed, coming in at the beginning, get rich with them.

So I don't propose you reject them out of hand. But how can you narrow the odds of them being in business in five to ten years time? How can you judge whether they will prosper?

Your first question: is it a pyramid?

Pyramids

Yes, I know they're illegal. But they're still around, wolves dressed in sheep's clothing, cleverly disguising themselves as honest network marketing schemes, often advertising themselves as groundfloor opportunities.

Here are the giveaway clues – and what you should do if you spot them.

- If the promoters pressure you to part with large sums of startup money as a **condition** of signing up (even if they claim it is for training sessions, computer services, etc.), be on your guard.
- If marketing a product or service to outside customers isn't central to the company's Marketing Plan, back off.

Re-read the section on pyramiding in Chapter 4 of this book if you're still in doubt.

Young companies

There will remain some new companies with an appealing product line, a punchy video, and attractive literature. You're interested. Why not? But unless you're a hopeless gambler or a complete sucker, there are some basic questions you should ask before signing up.

Here is a checklist you can use:

Financial stability. Find out as much as you can about the company's capital base, where the money comes from, and whether the company can walk away from its responsibilities if things go wrong, leaving you stranded. Some young networking operations are subsidiaries of subsidiaries of subsidiaries, the original money coming from an untouchable international conglomerate. If the operation collapses, you can be sure there'll be nobody you can successfully sue.

Secondly, a company without a sound financial base will not be able to pay its commission promptly, nor manage the rapid growth which it is doubtless promising you. Finally, look at the small print and make sure the buy-back guarantee is at least as good as you would get from a company in the DSA.

Risk. In business generally, it is accepted that risk is related to reward – and you are planning to invest in this new company because you hope to make money faster than with more conservative, longstanding ones. Even legitimate companies may encourage you to spend $1,500 upward on product inventory (for your own use and for sale to consumers and those you recruit) because it helps you on your way to the first rung of the company's ladder. In principle, I see nothing wrong with this, provided you are not pressured. It is a tiny investment compared with franchising or almost any other startup venture.

But there has to be a limit. Remember, in network marketing, the people you recruit will try to copy what you have done. How many people do you know with several thousand dollars to spare? How many people of the same sort will they know? You are limiting the potential size of your network immediately. Traditionally – and even today – the great attraction of network marketing is that you can get started for very little outlay.

Marketing plan. Does it give you the opportunity of making money at many levels? Is there any limit on your network size, and how much money you can make? Are you required to reach minimum target levels, month by month, just like salespeople with conventional companies? (For me, this would be a definite turnoff – it should be your own business, and your own choice of how hard you work). Is the concept simple (even if the Marketing Plan itself is complex)? Is your retail profit margin generous?

Training. How good are the sales aids? Is your sponsor keen to help you – and teach you how to teach others? Will there be meetings in your neighbourhood where you can introduce new people?

The product

When you've examined the company, think about the product. Whether it's a single product or a catalogue, there is a businesslike checklist you can go through.

Mass market. Is it something everyone could use – and want? Does it have universal appeal? If not, how big is its market? How many of your close family and friends would enjoy using it?

Market advantage. Does it have something genuinely new to offer? Is the product special? If it's so new that it has no track record, are you confident it will find a marketplace?

Reliability. Is it simple and usable, or hi-tech and complex? Is the company making false claims for its products? You don't want to find yourself with warranty or legal problems, or needing to go back to people's homes to fix what they have bought.

Pricing. Is it priced to sell? Is it good value? Will people think it a rip-off? What is its price compared to the competition?

Repeat sales. Is it consumable? That is to say, will a satisifed buyer come back automatically for more? If so, you will receive a passive income.

Crucially:

WILL YOU BUY AND USE IT YOURSELF?

As with any networking company, new or old, this to me is the key. You should feel instinctively that:

- You would like to try the product yourself
- The timing in the marketplace seems right
- Some of your friends would like to try it too

Caution. Finally, remember that the odds are against you. Most of these companies don't last. They are one-shot one-product businesses which may boom or bust. If you're a gambler – and that's your choice – by all means consider them.

But I believe there is a safer route which offers just as fast a journey to the top.

Which is: find a soundly-based, growing company with an established policy of offering groundfloor opportunities, through innovative product lines, at regular intervals. That way, you get the best of both worlds.

Safety plus opportunity

The most promising candidate here, in my view, is NSA®. Incorporated in Memphis, Tennessee, in 1970, as National Safety Associates of America, it has financial strength demonstrated in its excellent credit rating, and exceptional recent growth.

Its annual sales, combined with its sister company NSA International, are comfortably within the $100-500 million range, and this is putting the figure conservatively (see Box).

Any company which grows, in five years, from $5 million to over $350 million demands recognition (and explanation). During this period, it became an outstanding performer in Inc. Magazine's annual rating of the 500 fastest growing private companies in the U.S. For four consecutive years, from 1989 to 1992, NSA was in the top 100 – one of only two companies to achieve this.

One reason was undoubtedly its anticipation of the environmental boom. In the 70s and 80s (roughly the first 15 years of corporate life), it became the leading direct sales

---

FINANCIAL DISCLOSURE

One of the difficulties financial analysts have in comparing performance of network marketing companies is that published figures use different criteria. Amway, for instance, bases its $4 billion turnover on estimated retail value of sales.

NSA, by contrast, reports sales figures as those earned by the company net, after covering the costs of all payments to distributors. To compare the two, you might have to multiply NSA's figures by 1.8-2.0.

NSA is now one of only 15 companies belonging to the Direct Selling Association whose shares are publicly quoted, requiring higher levels of financial disclosure than privately held companies.

company in the US for smoke alarms, achieving $100m+ in sales.

Then the company looked at industries and new markets which were likely to grow to the year 2000 and beyond. Its president, Jay Martin, has set out his philosophy.

When I looked at where industry had been focused, decade by decade, I saw that in the '50s it had been plastics, in the '60s the space program, the '70s energy conservation, and the '80s computer technology.

There was no question in my mind that the number one concern in the '90s, and for many years after that, would be environmental and health concerns.

If you look back at the list of environmentally aware networking companies on pages 73–74, you will see that NSA is the only one with asterisks for all three main categories: air, water, and nutrition. In the first two, it has become market leader (its water treatment systems at one time outselling all other brands combined). Its unique nutritional product line, described more fully in the next chapter, was launched in 1993, and became an instant runaway success (see graph page 85), outpacing even the introduction of air and water products.

Underlying strategy

The would-be entrepreneur looking for groundfloor opportunities should look at the core aspect of NSA's business strategy.

NSA is above all a marketing company. It is in the business of moving attractive and saleable products from the manufacturer to the consumer. Sometimes NSA makes the product itself, sometimes it buys in from outside – whichever is the best business decision.

For new people thinking of becoming a distributor, the first important question is where NSA places itself within the product life cycle. Any commercial product has a life which mimics the life of a human being. It is introduced to the world, it grows, it reaches maturity, and eventually it declines. In graph form, it can be shown as a bell curve:

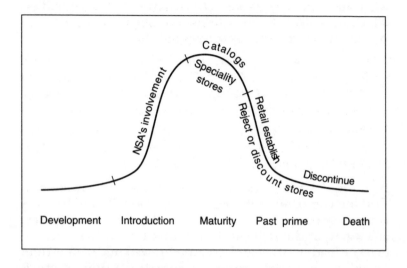

NSA, as a matter of policy, operates in the introductory stage of the product lifecycle, which is the most dynamic. In conventional marketing, it is also the riskiest and most expensive stage. Usually, huge sums of money have to be spent on advertising to make the product known, and there is customer resistance to be overcome. Because of this, most traditionally-based companies feel more comfortable coming into the market only when the product has a well-established track record.

But with good network marketing techniques, the opposite is true. The upside potential is enormous. With a new and original product, there is virtually no competition. An army of independent distributors themselves become the first customers, who then advertise the product painlessly by word of mouth. They make money because, at least for the initial introductory period, they have the field to themselves. They are able to generate a new generation of satisfied customers, some of whom in turn build their own marketing networks.

It is – to go back to the title of this chapter – a genuine groundfloor opportunity.

Moreover, NSA's track record during its 25-year history shows a remarkable improvement in its performance each time it has launched a new product. It started with fire detection equipment, moved on to water treatment units, followed these by air filters, and more recently introduced its pioneering nutritional line.

In each case it identified a new market opportunity and pounced on it before business as a whole was aware of the potential demand. As soon as it seemed that the products would soon become commonplace in the market, it had a new line ready to launch.

In my experience, this strategy is unparalleled in other networking companies, and NSA has confirmed that the strategy will remain in place in future years.

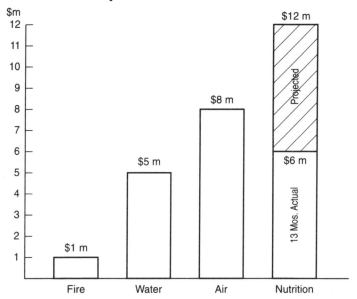

NSA product introduction

Sales of new product categories in $m per
month 2 years after introduction

NSA also believes that, compared with other networking companies, it has a higher proportion of seriously interested new people from the professions and from the business world. After visiting NSA's meetings in the United States, the UK, Germany, Holland, Belgium, and Switzerland, I think this to be true.

There was, of course, the cross-section of the population that you find everywhere in network marketing, people of all ages and types. Race, class, gender – these issues didn't matter.

But beyond the general enthusiasm, what impressed me was the number of experienced entrepreneurs who were taking an interest in NSA. I lost count of how many professionals I spoke to: businesspeople, lawyers, doctors, dentists, experts in financial services, accountants, bankers – they all told me that they were unlikely to see an opportunity like it in their lifetime, and that they were now committed.

WHERE DO YOU WANT TO BE?

David Stuckrath is one of NSA's high-flyers (they are given the title National Marketing Director, or NMD). After seven years, he has developed one of the largest organisations in the 10 countries where NSA presently does business.

20 years ago, shortly after college, I went into business for myself with a little bar and restaurant. At first, I was negative about MLM, but I kept bumping into average people who were making above-average incomes, and in January 1984 I joined them.

Since then, I've never looked back. NSA is my second company, and my last. I've achieved many of my goals, live in a beautiful home on the beach in Florida, and have two other residences. 18 months ago, I was semi- retired, with a great passive income. Then Juice Plus+ came along and recharged my excitement. I believe it is the most signficant nutritional product ever created. It has given me a new way of changing people's lives.

The men/women balance is also much more equal than in other meetings I went to, and other companies I researched. About half of the top earners are women, including Cheryl Cortese and Barbara Rebold, whose stories have been told in this book.

In 1993, NSA launched its fastest-selling product line to date. Called Juice Plus+™, some distributors became so enthusiastic after using it that they believed it might change the health pattern of a whole nation. It was, of course, much too soon to say that. But by year end, it seemed certain that for the fourth time in its history, NSA had hit upon a winner – and it was another groundfloor opportunity.

TIME WITH THE KIDS

Pam Popper, 37, from Columbus, Ohio, knows what it's like to work for yourself in the traditional way.

Into the office at 7 a.m., leave if you're lucky at 7 p.m., Monday through Saturday every week of the year. Borrowing and risking many dollars to make your business grow. If your kids are sick, you make arrangements for someone else to look after them. If they want you to take them on holiday, it's tough - you can't afford to leave your business to run itself, however successful.

Then, in January 1990, she took a closer look at network marketing.

The woman who introduced me to NSA was in the same business complex. I knew she was earning well, but she always seemed to have time to spare. A month later, I was completely hooked. I reached the top position in the company in a year, and the difference to my lifestyle was amazing. Positive cash flow meant no debts. I take the kids to school, exercise, start work around 10 or 11, have dinner with the family, and phone some friends in the evening. I travel, I have fun. Even the money is better. There's no comparison.

Chapter 10

A HEALTHY MARKET

Juice Plus+ is a remarkable product. It provides the benefits of juicing, and more, without the drawbacks. (Two drawbacks being, as anyone who bought a juicer knows, cost and time: the cost of large quantities of fresh fruit and vegetables, and the time spent chopping them into small pieces, and cleaning up the juicer when you've finished.)

Juice Plus+ was launched in the same month, April 1993, that the New York Times reported:

> *The United States Department of Agriculture has issued guidelines calling for a diet rich in vegetables and fruits, at least five servings a day. Few Americans, however, even come close to getting the minimum amount, according to a 1991 government study.*

Juice Plus+ easily gives you your five servings. It comes in capsules – two to be taken in the morning, two in the evening. The ingredients are entirely natural, with no sugar, starch, preservatives, synthetic colorants or chemical stabilizers.

The morning capsules are derived from fruits: mostly apple, orange, pineapple, and cranberry. The evening capsules are vegetable-based: carrots, barley, parsley, beets, kale, broccoli, cabbage, oats, and spinach.

The technological advance that has made this possible is the technique of flash-drying (see Box). The capsules are particularly rich in food enzymes that help your body absorb foodstuffs in your regular diet. According to an independent laboratory report, the enzyme content in a daily dose of Juice Plus+ is about the same as four pints of freshly-juiced fruit and vegetables.

Additionally, the capsules contain a balanced combination of soluble dietary fiber from several plant sources. They also contain food actives, or antioxidants, which many scientists now see as essential to health. A study by Dr. Joann Manson, of the Harvard Medical School, based on data collected since 1958, concluded:

A growing body of statistical evidence has shown the benefits of the so-called antioxidants A, C, and E. We found especially strong benefits of spinach and carrots, both potent sources of antioxidants. The research provides new support for the existing recommendation that people eat 5 servings of fruit and vegetables a day. People who ate carrots 5 times a week, for example, had a 68 per cent lower stroke risk than people who ate carrots once a month or less.

After the launch of Juice Plus+, sales exploded. In the first month, 2,000 cartons were sold. In December, the figure was 50,000 cartons – and the graph showed no signs of flattening. NSA's President, Jay Martin, commented:

It is without doubt the fastest-growing product line we have ever introduced – and it sits happily alongside the other products in our environmental catalogue.

HOW FLASH-DRYING WORKS

Juice Plus+ was developed in conjunction with NSA by Natural Alternatives International in Colorado Springs, Colo. While the precise process is proprietary information, the scientific breakthrough comes from removing liquid from fruit and vegetables at −90 degrees Centigrade.

Acording to the company: *The substance that remains is available for encapsulation. The juices are dried by us in a process which enables enzymes and the food properties to remain active – not destroyed, as they would be by boiling or evaporation.*

Trading history

In the early 1980s, US supermarkets were experiencing a new phenomenon. Shoppers, increasingly concerned at the taste of water coming out of their taps, were beginning to buy bottled water in quantity. It didn't seem to matter that carrying bottled water back home from the supermarket was inconvenient and (at around $1 a gallon) expensive. The purity was sometimes unreliable, and bottles were often a year old before they reached the supermarket shelf. Even so, shoppers kept on buying.

NSA's answer was to manufacture a water treatment unit that could be easily fitted in the home, and then forgotten. There must be no maintenance hassle, and no need to change filters. The unit also had to be highly cost-effective, compared to bottled water, over its 3-year life.

The product NSA came up with was named the 100S, a modest-sized cylinder, plumbed in under the kitchen sink, usually with its own special fountain tap. It enabled distributors to say:

> *Don't bother going shopping. We can clean up your water at home, fresh out of your taps. For a dollar a week, you will have as much clean water as you can possibly want.*

It took a while for the message to get through. To begin with, NSA used the same direct sales force as had been successfully selling smoke alarms. Sales, at less than $2m a year, were modest (to put it kindly).

Try it, you'll like it

Next, NSA adopted network marketing as a sales method. It helped somewhat. Sales increased. But the biggest jump happened when NSA introduced the idea of a free trial period for the product, with a demonstration countertop model. Distributors were encouraged tosay simply: *Try it, you'll like it*. A week later, they went back for the customer's reaction.

Ben Johnson, NSA's sales director in the days of smoke alarms, and still with the company today at the head of a network of 60,000 distributors, explains the impact:

HOW THE 100S WORKS

When you drink bottled water carried home from the super-market, the main reason it tastes better is because it contains little or no chlorine. This has often been removed by passing the water through a bed of granular activated carbon.

With an NSA bottled water unit, you are putting the water through the same process as many of the bottled water manufacturers, but at a fraction of the price. First, a screen mesh removes undissolved particles. Then, in the body of the filter, tiny activated carbon granules provide a large surface area to absorb the chlorine. The carbon is also impregnated with minute amounts of silver, to help prevent bacteria growing within the unit.

Colossal. People borrowed a filtration unit for a week, and suddenly they could taste for themselves what good clean water was, without the chlorine which all the water companies put in. It also opened up a whole new world of distributors. 5% of people have sales skills, 95% don't. With NSA's approach, you can turn the figures the other way round. 95% of people find it absolutely natural to lend something they themselves enjoy. Why not? Lending and sharing are part of normal life.

NSA had hit on the marketing formula that worked. It led to liftoff. An article in *Woman's Own* magazine went so far as to forecast: *Water filters will be the next standard kitchen appliance.*

Today, NSA's catalogue abounds with variations on the original clean-water concept: for instance, devices that produce sparkling water, and refrigerated clean water for offices.

The air market

After water came air. Again, NSA hit on a hot market. The dangers of passive smoking are universally known. Indoor air, where we spend 95% of our time, is up to 20 times more polluted than outdoors. Air conditioning systems, particularly old ones, simply re-circulate contaminated air.

NSA decided that the market was for filtration systems which would physically remove microscopic particles of dust and bacteria, and also absorb and neutralize most gases and odors. Rather than develop a system or systems from scratch, NSA hunted down state-of-art scientific technology which could be built into units which they would manufacture themselves.

Future growth

At the same time, NSA was expanding internationally, opening up new territories into which US distributors could build their networks. By spring 1994, NSA was operating in nine countries: the US, Canada, Mexico, the

---

HOW AIR FILTERS WORK

A "micron" is the unit used to measure dirt particles in the air. It is one-millionth of a meter. About 400 would fit on the dot of this letter i.

All bacteria, insecticide dust, animal dander, and smoke particles, are smaller than a micron. So NSA had to find a filtration system that would be effective down to these microscopic levels.

The small-unit filters collect anything larger than 0.3 microns. For the large-room or office filters, NSA went even further. They use what is known as HEPA filtration ("High Efficiency Particulate Air"), which is effective to 0.1 microns.

This filter, developed by the US military, and used by the Atomic Energy Commission for removing radioactive dust from underground sites, cleans air to the standards required by hospital operating theatres and burns units. (You need an electron microscope to see a particle as small as 0.1 micron in size; even viruses are generally larger than this).

---

4 REASONS FOR JOINING

David Sage, with a worldwide distribution network of over 20,000, admits that his success with NSA is bound to make him enthusiastic about the company.

But the fact is that I researched more than 200 companies before choosing NSA, and the four reasons that brought me here are as valid today as when I first joined in 1987.

1. The right people run the company. NSA's leadership showed a higher level of commitment than any other company I looked at.
2. The product line is right. NSA chooses and develops products where there is both a significant and recognized need.
3. The timing is right. NSA has a unique balance of longterm stability and current opportunity that you don't usually have with either a startup or a long-established company.
4. The marketing plan is right. NSA offers new and old distributors unlimited potential, financial freedom, and the opportunity to make a difference.If your desire to succeed is strong enough, if you are single-minded and persistent, and if you're looking for a vehicle to take you to your destination, I can only say that NSA is the best set of wheels on the road.

UK, Ireland, Germany, Holland, Belgium, Switzerland and France. Italy would follow, and then the rest of Europe. Distributors in the company's home town of Memphis were told:

> *It is sometimes difficult for us here in the United States to imagine that the market in Europe, when you include all those countries newly freed from Russia, is three times the size of our own. If you're in network marketing, and you know just one person speaking the local tongue, you can be there.*

Since the introduction of Juice Plus+, NSA's catalogue is better-balanced. Previously it contained mostly high-ticket items. Now it is possible to make a start with inexpensive inventory, and move up from there. I believe that if you want to build a seriously large networking business, NSA is the best opportunity I have come across.

Conculsion

Perhaps the strangest thing that newcomers to network marketing find, coming as they often do straight from the dog-eat-dog world of commercial business, is that everyone wishes you well, and encourages you to succeed.

Partly this is because the field is wide open. Because saturation, in practice, can never remotely happen, there is simply no need to compete. But more than that, *the system rewards the basic human urge to help others. When you do, you prospe*r.

There is a famous description of this:

> *You can have anything in the world that you want, simply by helping enough other people to get what they want.*

The founders of network marketing may not have realized at the time what they were doing, but they wedded two of the most powerful forces in the human psyche. We like to get, and we like to give. It's a happy and unusual marriage.

The result, most people discover when they join network marketing, is a camaraderie unlike any other form of business. At meetings, you come face to face with dozens of successful people all urging you to be equally successful. Your network takes on a life of its own. It's exciting, and it can be rewarding.

Just one final word. Network marketing is thriving, and the environmental market is expanding. With or without you, they are boom businesses that are happening right now.

Appendix

CODE OF ETHICS
PREAMBLE

The Direct Selling Association, recognizing that companies engaged in direct selling assume certain responsibilities toward consumers arising out of the personal-contact method of distribution of their products and services, hereby sets forth the basic fair and ethical principles and practices to which member companies of the Association will continue to adhere in the conduct of their business.

A. CODE OF CONDUCT

1. Deceptive or Unlawful Consumer Practices

No member company of the Association shall engage in any deceptive, unlawful, or unethical consumer or recruiting practice.

2. Products or Services

The offer of products or services for sale by member companies of the Association shall be accurate and truthful as to price, grade, quality, make, value, performance, quantity currency of model, and availability.

3. Terms of Sale

A written order or receipt shall be delivered to the customer at the time of sale, which sets forth in language that is clear and free of ambiguity:

A. All the terms and conditions of sale, with specification of the total amount the customer will be required to pay, including all interest, service charges and fees, and other costs and expenses as required by federal and state law.

B. The name and address of the salesperson or the member firm represented.

4. Warranties and Guarantees

The terms of any warranty or guarantee offered by the seller in connection with the sale shall be furnished to the buyer in a manner that fully conforms to federal and state warranty and guarantee laws and regulations.

The manufacturer, distributor and/or seller shall fully and promptly perform in accordance with the terms of all warranties and guarantees offered to consumers.

5. Pyramid Schemes

For the purpose of this Code, pyramid or endless chain schemes shall be considered consumer transactions actionable under this Code. The Code Administrator shall determine whether such pyramid or endless chain schemes constitute a violation of this code in accordance with applicable federal, state and/or local law or regulation.

6. Inventory Repurchase

Any member company with a marketing plan that involves selling products directly or indirectly to independent salespeople shall clearly state, in its recruiting literature or contract with the independent salespeople, that the company will repurchase on reasonable commercial terms currently marketable inventory in the possession of that salesperson and purchased by that salesperson for resale prior to the date of termination of the salesperson's business relationship with the company or its independent salespeople.

For purposes of this Code, "reasonable commercial terms" shall include the repurchase of marketable inventory within 12 months from the salesperson's date of purchase at not less than 90% of the salesperson's original net cost less appropriate setoffs and legal claims, if any. For purposes of this Code, products shall not be considered "currently marketable" if returned for repurchase after the products' commercially reasonable usable or shelf-life period has passed; nor shall products be considered "currently marketable" if the company clearly discloses to salespeople prior to purchase that the products are seasonal, discontinued, or special promotion products and are not subject to the repurchase obligation.

7. Earnings Representations

No member company shall misrepresent the actual or potential sales or earnings of its independent salespeople. Any earnings or sales representations that are made by member companies shall be based on documented facts.

The above extracts Copyright © Direct Selling Association 1992 reprinted by kind permission of the DSA.